Lyle Stuart on Baccarat

Books by Lyle Stuart

Casino Gambling for the Winner (1978)
God Wears a Bow Tie (a novel)
Inside Western Union (with M. J. Rivise)
Lyle Stuart on Baccarat (1984)
Mary Louise (a love story)
The Secret Life of Walter Winchell
Winning at Casino Gambling (1996)

Lyle Stuart

on

Baccarat

Barricade Books

Published by Barricade Books Inc.
150 Fifth Avenue
Suite 700
New York, NY 10011

Printed in the United States of America.

Library of Congress Cataloging-in-Publication Data

Stuart, Lyle.
    Lyle Stuart on baccarat.
        p.   cm.
    Originally published: Secaucus. N.J.: L. Stuart, c1984.
    ISBN 1-56980-105-3
    1. Baccarat. 2. Gambling.   I. Title.
    GV1295.B3S78   1997
    795.4'2—dc21   96-44078
                                                           CIP

10 9 8 7 6 5 4 3 2 1

Proem

Gambling is a personal matter. Therefore, this book, like its 1984 predecessor on which it is built, is a personal narrative with splashes of autobiographical experience. These come from days and nights of sitting at baccarat tables and the other table games in gambling casinos throughout the world.

That's how I wrote my previous gaming books, and they've become leaders in the field. Why tamper with a winning formula?

I would like to thank the people who have given of their time to read the manuscript of this book and to make suggestions for its improvement. They include the ever-faithful Arnold Bruce Levy, my good friend Victor Lownes, my beautiful wife Carole, and my dearly beloved daughter Sandra Lee.

Contents

Introduction

Gamblers are fools, and any fool can attempt to write a gambling book. Since my original *Casino Gambling for the Winner*, which I wrote in 1978, hundreds of fools have tried. A few have succeeded in having books published that are embarrassments to anyone who knows and understands the guts of gaming.

Lyle Stuart on Baccarat was the first book to deal with the game of baccarat seriously. It was written with a savvy only a seasoned player could acquire.

Perhaps that's part of why it has become a classic.

Lyle Stuart on Baccarat eventually went out of print. Over a period of time, its publishing house (which I owned and eventually sold for $12 million) was forced to return orders for hundreds of copies.

We didn't go back to press because I believe in giving readers value for their money, and the book had become dated.

Recently, I won two baccarat tournaments in Atlantic City.

The two tournaments, one at what was then Bally's Grand (now the Hilton) and one at Donald Trump's Taj Mahal, gave me a combined win of $245,000.

News of my two victories stimulated an even-greater demand for my out-of-date baccarat book. A man in Japan offered me $1,000 if I could locate a copy for him.

One thousand dollars for one copy of my book! Here was every book publisher's dream!

I forgot Pearl Harbor long enough to send the man one of my few remaining personal copies with my compliments.

And I knew the time had come to rewrite and update. Thus this book.

Lyle Stuart
Stuyvesant, NY 12173
April 16, 1997

Baccarat

Zero!

Nothing!

Yes, that's the literal translation of the Italian word *baccara*—and that's how the name of the game originated.

It's the richest gambling game in any casino. Last year, there were only eighty-two fourteen-seat baccarat tables in twenty-six locations in the entire state of Nevada. Of these, sixty-one were located in casinos on the Las Vegas Strip. These were surrounded by 1,600 other table games, ranging from blackjack, craps, and Pow Gai to Let-'em-Ride and Caribbean poker. Yet these eighty-two tables produced a win for the casinos of $461,695,000. By comparison, during the same period, 3,560 blackjack tables in 204 locations yielded

$988,770,000, and 464 craps tables in 146 locations produced a win of $393,521,000.

In other words, those few baccarat tables generated more than one-third of the "hold" (winnings) on all table games.

In 1997, with new casinos opening, the number increased to eighty-seven tables.

Atlantic City, by contrast, currently has thirty-two baccarat tables in ten of its twelve casinos. (Harrah's Marina doesn't offer the game, and the Claridge closed its single baccarat table.)

To give you clues to where the action is, these are the total baccarat wins for each casino for the year ending December 31, 1996:

Atlantic City Hilton	$5,822,238
Bally's Park Pace	$3,573,082
Caesars	$29,653,384
Claridge	$40,073
Resorts	$4,746,711
Sands	$10,832,988
Showboat	$7,209,122
Tropicana	$7,977,262
Trump Castle	$5,917,605
Trump Plaza	$5,784,277
Trump Taj Mahal	$47,687,354

In 1996, these thirty-two tables generated a win of $129,244,096. This includes months when some of them had to report net losses.

The month of December win was the largest in the

history of gaming in Atlantic City. The casinos netted $3,789,350,761. This, after deducting $3,150,613 for uncollectible patrons' checks.

Oddly, this rosy picture isn't as glowing as it appears. In the 1996 marketing war, Atlantic City gave away so many rolls of quarters and spent so much on promotional giveaways and perks that profits fell by almost 20 percent.

Atlantic City casinos spent $615 million to attract customers. Only two casinos, Trump Plaza and Caesars Atlantic City increased their profits from the previous year. Nothing grows to the sky, and both Vegas and Atlantic City will eventually face the law of diminishing returns.

But weep not for the casinos. Weep for the customers. They're not playing on level fields. The casinos are not at risk except at baccarat tables.

Baccarat is the *only* table game that can severely hurt a casino. That's why 1996 saw this smallest growth in casino winnings in years. Casino owners attribute it to the major drop in baccarat winnings.

How does Atlantic City's win compare with Nevada's? Despite the drop in baccarat winnings, Nevada's 362 casinos won $7.4 billion. Impressive until you learn that Atlantic City's twelve casinos won nearly $4 billion. That's more than half of what was won in all Nevada!

But Nevada and Atlantic City have more to be concerned about than each other. There's the proliferation of riverboat casinos and Native American casinos. There's the fact that many high rollers are going to other parts of the world for their fun and games. Australian casinos are thriving. And in Seoul, South Korea, the huge casino can't expand its gaming area fast enough to accommodate the eager punters.

To give you some notion of the worldwide explosion of casino gambling, only one American hotel, the MGM Grand, has more rooms (5,005) than the Ambassador City in Jomtien, Thailand, with its 4,631 rooms.

Fortunes are won and lost in baccarat on the turn of four, five, or six cards.

I mean *fortunes*.

Kerry Packer
Strikes Again!

Australia's wealthiest man, Kerry Francis Bullmore Packer, visited the baccarat pit in the MGM Grand in Las Vegas. He alternated with a little quarter-of-a-million-dollar-a-hand blackjack. In less than two hours, he left the casino with $24 million of what had been the MGM Grand's money.

One result? The top executives at the MGM Grand, including capable president Larry Woolf, were fired summarily by owner Kirk Kerkorian. But not until a casino executive was flown to Australia to tell Packer, face to face, that his gaming action was no longer welcome at the MGM Grand.

The innovative Woolf, while president, constructed two private baccarat rooms. Between them, he built a resting lounge with comfortable sofas, right in the heart of the casino.

You can walk through the 171,000 square feet of the MGM Grand's gambling area and even saunter into the baccarat pit, and you'd never know that lounge was there, hidden from all public view.

It took imagination and courage to devote this much space to a seeming nonrevenue-producing area, but Woolf knew exactly what he was doing. Big players moved from the Mirage to the MGM Grand.

Also when he was president, Woolf searched the country for the best restaurant in America. He settled on Chicago's Charlie Trotter's. He duplicated it and then some in a restaurant designed exclusively for high rollers. (My wife and I were Woolf's dinner guests two nights before the executive firings and can testify that it was, indeed, the best restaurant in all of Las Vegas.)

No sooner did Woolf depart the premises than the new MGM chairman, J. Terrence Lanni, closed Charlie Trotter's. Perhaps it was too much a reminder of the Woolf* administration. Lanni also cut credit limits and fired 770 casino employees.

A year before, the MGM Grand had won $132 million from its baccarat pit, but that was quickly forgotten.

Casino operators of the old school would not have become frantic by a temporary loss—even one of more than $20 million. But Kirk Kerkorian is not a gambler. He's a wheeler-dealer who enjoys adding to his fortune.

---

*On leaving the MGM Grand, Larry Woolf formed the Navegante Group, a consulting company. A short while later, he supervised the opening of Casino Niagara in Ontario, on the Canadian side of Niagara Falls.

He isn't willing to lose millions on the flip of a few cards by a lucky customer.

Kerkorian, who owns 72 percent of all available MGM Grand stock, rarely eats at any of his hotel's nine gourmet restaurants. Rather, he dines at a modest eatery, where he prefers to go unnoticed. At his beach house in Malibu, California, he sleeps in the guest bedroom rather than in the master bedroom. In other words, he has a gift for accumulating money, but little talent for spending it.

Getting back to the colorful Kerry Packer, not too long after the incident described above, Packer took six million from the Mirage. This was one that Steve Wynn lost.

Packer bets a mite bit heavier than you or I. His maximum bet is often $250,000, and sometimes he plays every hand for nothing less than that amount.

Packer is shrewd. He knows that baccarat offers the best odds of all table games.

Casino Owners

Casino owners are not gamblers. The players aren't supposed to win. Still, greed often makes it seem attractive to welcome action from the "whales," those high rollers who can lose a million or more on a visit.

The shock that follows when a whale swallows millions of the casino's money is difficult for the owners to digest.

Gaming Today reported that in the last quarter of 1996, the Las Vegas Hilton suffered such large losses in its baccarat pit that Harry Curtis, a vice president and senior analyst for the Wall Street firm of Smith Barney, lowered his earnings estimate for Hilton Hotels Corporation stock from 33 cents to 29 cents a share.

The Associated Press attributed a $68,100,000 loss to "a cold streak at the Las Vegas Hilton baccarat tables and little compensating action at the [Hilton] Laughlin and Reno casinos."

The Las Vegas Hilton caters to several hundred high-wagering baccarat players from all over the world. The casino recently spent $12 million on a luxury baccarat pit for their biggest gamblers. And for good reason: baccarat winnings usually make up 70 to 80 percent of that casino's revenue.

How important is gambling to Hilton? Very. Hilton is now the largest casino operator in the world. Gambling earnings are twice the revenue that Hilton receives from all of its 264 franchised hotels.

Baccarat can equal BIG money!

Last New Year's Eve, a single player is said to have lost $10 million playing baccarat at Caesars Tahoe, even while a group of Asians won $5 million in the same casino. The New Year's weekend is considered the biggest high-roller gathering of the year. Michael J. Goodman, writing in the *Los Angeles Times* magazine, quotes casino bosses calling it "their annual trek to Mecca."

When Arthur Goldberg moved from heading Bally's to become president of the Hilton Hotels Corporation casinos, he bluntly announced that the party was over. "We will offer gambling, but we will not be gambling ourselves."

When pressed for an explanation, he explained that there will be stricter (small) betting limits.

It was a move that would discourage high-roller baccarat players. What would Hilton do with its four 15,000-square-foot luxury suites built in 1995 at a cost of $50 million? These came with satin-and-gold draperies and usually with a private chef.

Oh, well. Goldberg could fill the rooms with broken promises. He broke one to me when he ran Bally's Grand in Atlantic City, and I never played there again.

If baccarat offers the most favorable odds in a casino, you should know that this is only one reason owners are nervous about it. Michael J. Goodman quotes one top casino executive in his article as saying, "That's where the stomach for this comes in. You've got to be able to give credit instantly under conditions no bank would follow: no collateral, based largely upon reputation. If the customer wins $6 million, he leaves with the cash. If he comes back and loses $6 million, it's credit. You'll be happy—glad—to call it even if you get $5 million back over the next year or so."

My Promise

If baccarat offers the best (lowest) odds against you, the next best wagers are the Pass line and the Don't Pass line in craps. The dice game takes 1.41 percent of your wager.*

---

*I'm talking here about the normal course of things. There are those who argue that when casinos give double odds, five times odds, and ten times odds, the casino's edge shrinks. In theory, when played into infinity, neither the player nor the casino will profit on free odds.

At this writing, 100 times odds is available in Las Vegas at both Binion's Horseshoe on Fremont Street and the Stratosphere on the Strip. Bet $1 on the Pass line and the 100 times free odds ($100) behind the line and you have shrunk the casino edge from 1.41 to .002

Baccarat offers odds of only 1.06 against your Bank side wager or 1.23 if you chose to bet on the Player side. (The casino evens out the difference by charging the so-called "commission" on winning Bank bets. More on that later.)

In the pages that follow, I'll tell you everything I've learned about baccarat. (The first thing you should know is that the "t" in baccarat is silent. You pronounce the name of the game *bah-cah-rah*.)

I'll share with you what I know about the rules, regulations, and money management. I'll tell you everything I know to give you the best possible chance to enter the Winner's Circle.

---

percent. That means the casino will collect a little more than two cents on your combined wager.

It's partly an illusion, of course. The megamultiple-odds bet is a casino ploy. They look upon the free odds as something that won't generate a profit or a loss, but they still look at your Pass line bet as being 1.41 percent in their favor.

Why then do casinos do it? Competition, primarily. It's a great lure. The fact is the casino wants you to make a Pass line bet or a Don't Pass bet. Those are the ones that will bring in the money to pay the electric bill. At this writing, every casino in Atlantic City has select tables where you can wager five-times free odds. This cuts the casino edge to 1.85 percent and gives them one penny for each ten dollars you wager. Incidentally, for those who believe slot machines are the cash cows for casinos, take note that Binion's Horseshoe recently removed some slots to make room for a second baccarat table.

I can't promise to make you a winner. Only you can make you a winner. But I promise to give you more knowledge of the game than some players have whom I've watched bet $25,000 and $50,000 a hand.

Fair enough?

The Beginnings

Black-tie baccarat, as we know it today, originated in Cuba. The origins of the game it derives from were in the courts of Europe in the Middle Ages. There are indications that a game of nines was played in the court of Louis XIV sometime around the year 1680. Other sources say the game originated among the pimps of the Paris ghetto. Still others say it was born on the island of Corsica.

The game of *chemin de fer* probably originated in Italy. When it was embraced by Louis XIV and his French aristocrats in the seventeenth century, many became such devotees that after the French Revolution, Napoleon branded it a game of the nobility and attempted to suppress it.

Shimmy, as it was nicknamed in America, required

decisions by both players and banker. By contrast, American baccarat is an automatic game. No decisions. It is played according to a standard set of rules.

In 1958, Francis "Tommy" Renzoni was a casino executive at the Hotel Capri in Havana. The casino was named "George Raft's" to honor the famous gangster-playing movie actor after whom so many real gangsters modeled themselves. His face was on the chips.

Raft himself received no share of the profits. The casino was owned, nominally at least, by Dino Cellini. The Cellini brothers were, as the underworld wise guys like to say, "connected." They were part of the Meyer Lansky organization.

Lansky himself was not a gambler. He'd play golf with former *Variety* managing editor Nat Kahn for two dollars a game. He'd sulk whenever he lost the two dollars.

Lansky was referred to affectionately among associates as "the little man."* He had, long ago, learned that the money in casinos was no gamble if you were on the

---

*Lansky was cheap. A year after his associate, Abner "Longy" Zwillman hung himself in his New Jersey attic, Longy's stepson flew to Florida for his honeymoon.

The mob fraternity, many of its elder members enjoying retirement, threw a party at a Miami Beach restaurant to welcome the newlyweds.

A collection of wedding gifts was made of envelopes containing cash. The envelopes contained varying amounts ranging up to $3,000.

Lansky's envelope wasn't among the others. He took

casino side. All one needed were players who played long enough to be ground out by the per. ("The per" is the percentage in favor of the house. The per is locked into every bet made at casino tables except, as explained earlier, for the one wager at craps called "free odds.")

It was nearly midnight of New Year's Eve 1959. Tommy Renzoni wasn't working in the casino. Instead, he was supervising a high-stakes craps game on the mattress in his suite at Havana's Hotel Capri.

Sometimes, before the dice were tossed, as much as $200,000 was piled on the white sheets. The dice were being tossed against a pillow at the head of the bed.

Tension was high, and the players were noticeably annoyed when the phone rang.

Tommy held up his hand to halt the game while he answered.

The voice at the other end was one which Tommy

Zwillman's son aside and whispered, "Meet me tomorrow at six in the morning at the park across from the hotel. I'll have something for you."

The son hardly slept in anticipation of what he believed would be a generous gift from his father's former partner.

At 6 A.M., Lansky was in the park, seated on a bench.

"Not here," he told the eager young man, "someone may be watching."

After looking in all directions, they walked a few

didn't recognize. "Tommy, get out of the country! Castro has won. Batista is getting out. You get out."

Only days before, Cuban dictator Fulgencio Batista, flanked by his smiling American military advisers, held a televised news conference at which he ridiculed the idea that Fidel Castro and his raggedy rebels posed any threat to his American-backed government.

So Tommy Renzoni felt he had the right to be angry at the interruption. "Listen, pal," he muttered into the mouthpiece of his phone, "keep your April Fool's jokes for April. I'm in the middle of a big game."

He slammed down the receiver.

The shooter picked up the dice. Excitement mounted. The point was four.

The shooter was about the toss the dice when the phone rang again.

Visibly annoyed, Tommy grabbed it again. But before he could utter the chain of expletives on the tip of his tongue, the deep voice at the other end spoke in Sicilian.

---

blocks. Then Lansky handed the young man an envelope.

"I couldn't wait to get back to our hotel room to show my bride what I assumed was the big gift," Longy Zwillman's son told me. "Imagine my surprise when we opened the envelope and it contained $250. My father sometimes tipped waiters that much."

At the time, newspaper articles speculated on Lansky's personal wealth, reported to be hidden in Swiss banks. The amounts ranged from $100 million to $300 million.

This was no joke. Value your life? Get out of Cuba. Now! Get a ship. Get a plane. But get out tonight.

Tommy didn't leave immediately. He hung around for several months so that he could appear before a revolutionary committee to persuade its members that the American money in his safe deposit box was legitimate and should be returned to him. It was returned, but in Cuban pesos rather than U.S. dollars. Renzoni converted these to American dollars on the black market at the going rate, which was ten pesos for one American dollar.

After they made their triumphant entrance into Havana, the casinos were closed by Fidel Castro and his *barbudos*. Three months later, Castro reversed himself. He realized that casinos were necessary to attract the now-scarce American tourists.

Tommy evaluated the situation. Gambling was going to be government regulated, and Cubans would be in charge.

Now it really was time to go. He packed his things and three days after the casinos reopened, was en route to Nevada via Miami.

He took with him his wife, his three children, and some pleasant memories of a Havana that had been the Paris of the Western Hemisphere. He left behind one uncompleted dice hand, several frustrated players, and at least one safe deposit box containing two hundred thousand American dollars which he hadn't reported to the committee because he wanted his dollars rather than pesos.

Later, as a journalist, I became friendly with Fidel

Castro and Che Guevara.* After Tommy learned this, he had a running gag with me. "Listen, Lyle, next time you see your friends in Havana, ask if they'll give me back my two hundred grand."

If Tommy had retrieved his $200,000, chances are strong that he would have gambled and lost it all at baccarat.

---

*At the time, Che headed the Cuban National Bank. For reasons that don't belong in a book about gambling, he became one of my heroes. Today my automobile license plate reads simply: CHE.

The Origins

Nobody really knows the name of the mathematical genius who devised the game of baccarat. Like Topsy remarked in *Uncle Tom's Cabin*, it probably "just growed."

The original game was a pure matter of heads or tails. Each side received two cards. Each side had to make a decision on whether to take a third card.

Gradually the rules changed. Whether or not the dealer gave Player a third card began to be decided by a set of fixed rules. These rules gave the player discretion to draw or not to draw a third card only if the first two cards totaled five.

The game was known as *chemin de fer*, and it was a game of player against player, with the house collecting a commission.

The Greeks had a name for it three-quarters of a century ago in 1922, and the name of the variation they created was *à deux tableaux*. This meant that they were
dealing from one shoe to two players.

The banker of the famous Greek game played on the
French Riviera in the 1920s was a man named Nick
Zographos. He sat in the middle and played his hand
against both sides of the table. This made for some
interesting decisions.

Nick was a founding member of what came to be
called "The Greek Syndicate." This consisted of a quar-
tet of daring men from Athens who would study both
Player hands. Nick would measure the size of the bets.
He would then speculate on what hand each side had,
depending on whether the players had called for a card
(the third card was dealt face up) or whether the player
stood pat.

Often Nick wouldn't draw, even though the rules
allowed him to and even though he knew it meant his
certain loss to one side. This because he calculated that
he could beat the hand on the side of the table where the
most money was wagered.

A variation, of course, was for the shoe to move
around the table with a player putting up a sum of money
as the shoe came to his position. He would announce the
amount of his bank. The person to his right covered what
he wanted to. The next person covered more. And so on,
until either all the players had wagered or the amount put
up by the banker had been matched. Then the person
with the shoe would deal from it.

If he won, the house would take 5 percent of his winnings. In dramatic confrontation, a player would call

"*banco*," meaning that he would match the entire amount being wagered by the banker that hadn't already been "covered" (bet against).

A disadvantage of this game was that you couldn't always bet a bundle. Your possible winnings were limited by the amount of money the banker would put up or the amount of money the players were willing to bet against the bank.

Nevertheless, since it was "the only game in town," it attracted men and women of great wealth. But the average player in Bad Homburg or Monte Carlo preferred the easier-to-understand challenge of the roulette wheel.

The European game traveled across the sea, first to Argentina and then to Havana. At the time, Americans considered Cuba an American colony. Earlier I referred to it as the Paris of the Western Hemisphere. It was also the whorehouse of the Western world. In this atmosphere, gambling flourished.

There were crooked casinos and crooked national lotteries. Batista and his cronies became inordinately wealthy. One of his associates, Rolando Masferrer, impatient with the slow grind of the casinos, had a more direct solution to his money needs. When Masferrer wanted cash, he drove to the Cuban treasury building accompanied by armed members of his private thousand-man army. His aides carried in empty suitcases which they filled with newly printed 100-peso notes.

Even casino owners have to work harder than that for their money.

Americans were delightful lollipops. They visited the notorious Shanghai Theater to ogle the round-the-clock stag movies and the live sex acts. (In the lobby of the theater was a huge religious statue of Madonna and Child.)

They thronged to the nightclub that featured "Superman" in action. The man filling the "Superman" role had a huge, perpetually erect penis and was Havana's hero for about six months.*

Americans visited the Havana houses of prostitution and the B-bars such as Club Mambo and the Blue Moon, where women of every age, shape, and hue were plentiful and cheap. And American tourists filled the casinos until the crowds were so thick that some players were blocked from placing their bets.

It was noisy, and it was fun. The wheels were gimmicked (fixed) so that, like Humphrey Bogart ordering it by saying "Have you tried twenty-two?" to a forlorn young man in a scene in the movie classic *Casablanca*, a number could be "forced" by the croupier, pressing a hidden button or stepping on a lever.

Blackjack was dealt by "mechanics," men who could deal "seconds" indefinitely which even the sharpest eyes and ears couldn't detect. The customary policy, as for example at Havana's Tropicana casino, was to deal honestly until the player made his big bet. It was then that the mechanic took control of the deck.

Word came of a new variation of baccarat that had

---

*Eventually the drug "Superman" took to maintain the erection lost its effectiveness, and then he discovered, to his horror, that he could never have an erection again. The fallen Superman became a lonely, tragic figure, wandering the streets of Old Havana, even as the tourists celebrated his successor.

been introduced in Argentina. With a few slight changes, it was introduced in Havana and became known as "Cuban baccarat."

The game developed to fill a need. It was an automatic game. You could bet on Bank or Player, and the casino booked all the bets. The dealing was strictly according to rules. There were no options, except deciding how much to bet and which side to bet on. All else was automatic and pure chance. It was a mindless game.

The game caught on. Not too successfully at first, but on some good nights, the house reaped profits of $50,000 to $100,000 from the baccarat table. This placated the owners for the barren times—those nights when nobody came to play.

Oddly enough, although gimmicked gaming shoes had already been developed in Cuba just ninety miles away, when the game reached America, baccarat was honest.

True, at first there were a few crude attempts to stack cards to favor the Player or Bank side, but since the customers could wager on either side, no one could anticipate how the customers would bet. A result was that the house would often get strangled in a streak of its own making.*

---

*This reminds me of a junket from New York to one of the Caribbean islands. The house introduced its own shaved (crooked) dice into the game twenty minutes before departure time. But the players kept switching so rapidly from Pass to Don't Pass, and back again, that afterwards one of the owners complained, "You Americans can't be trusted. We got

taken for forty 'big ones' [$40,000] with our own
gaffed cubes!"
I mention this because a casino could cheat at baccarat. However, cheating is unlikely in large casinos
in Nevada and New Jersey. They don't need to
cheat. Unless you learn to hit-and-run, they're going
to take most of your money anyway.
If you are so unsophisticated about casino gambling
that this news comes as a surprise to you, then do
yourself and your bankroll a favor and stay home.

Expensive Entertainment

You didn't buy this book to have me persuade you not to gamble, but I'll try anyway.

Frank Rich of the *New York Times* observed recently that "America is punch drunk with gambling."

Want to know my feelings about gambling? I quote Victor Lownes. He ran London's Playboy Casino when it was the most profitable casino in the world. Lownes insists that gambling is nothing more or less than "expensive entertainment."

It's slightly more complicated than that. Until a few years ago, if you ran a gambling casino anywhere in the United States outside of Nevada, you risked arrest and imprisonment. In other words, society looked upon casino gambling as racketeering. Casino gambling is still nothing more than a racket, except that now it is legal in many states and on Indian ("Native American") reservations.

Casinos offer sophisticated ways to separate you from your money. As casinos have proliferated, many thousands of men and women have become casino addicted and have destroyed their own lives and often those of their families. Casino gambling has caused hundreds of suicides and broken up thousands of homes. It has stunted educational budgets for children, etc.

The *Montgomery* (Alabama) *Advertiser* observed that gambling is "a transfer of money from the lower-middle income and poor to the casino operators."

Our government's obligation is to protect its citizens. Instead, many state governments are coconspirators with their phony lotteries, which prey upon the poorest among us.

When you read that casinos will add so many *billion* dollars a year to a state's economy, keep in mind that this money is not an accumulation of pennies from heaven. It's taken out of the pockets of the rich, the middle class, and the poor.

In Atlantic City, they actually run buses from the poorest sections of Harlem and Spanish Harlem on the day the postal service delivers welfare checks. Nobody is immune. And, to quote the brother-in-law of Joe W. Brown, the oilman who, for a time, owned Binion's Horseshoe in Las Vegas, "We haven't done our jobs until the customer's last check bounces."

In short, the casino owners want your last penny.

Most people who gamble and lose only vaguely

know the rules. They are usually totally unsophisticated about the odds. People lose huge amounts of money without ever understanding the percentages against them.

One of the interesting findings of gambling studies is that when casinos open in an area, those people who live closest to them are most likely to be the most frequent visitors—and losers. Those who live further away make fewer journeys to the slots and tables.

I know several men who have spent their entire adult lives working in the casino business. They've lived eight hours a day for twenty and thirty years in casinos. They've dealt, supervised, handled credit, and listened to sad stories.

They've seen everything there is to see about gambling.

Not one of them could tell me that he knew a single player who has won money over any extended period of time. Not one in thirty years!

Not *one*!

Believe this. It is truth.

Short-term wins? Sure. But the owners consider these merely temporary high-interest loans. The winners will return and play and play until they lose it all back—and more.

Casinos are not in the charity business.

Betting systems are a delusion. They're fed by the wishful fantasy that you can get something for nothing. The probability is more likely that you'll get nothing for your something.

If there were systems that could beat a casino game, they would have been revealed and made inoperative by the casinos a long time ago.

You can't avoid that *per*. That inexorable percentage against you is in every flop of the cards, every toss of the dice, every spin of the wheel, and every pull on the slot machine.

If you are still prepared to risk your money on casino games, know that time at the tables is against you. Know that with time, the percentage is absolutely guaranteed to make you a loser.

And never, but never, say I didn't warn you!

Think about it. Gambling produces nothing. No one in the casino halls makes a product. The gaming action simply siphons money from other parts of the economy.

You are entertained, but there's nothing you can wrap up and take home to the wife and kiddies.

More money is now gambled in casinos than is taken in for *all* the sports events, *all* the rock concerts, *all* the movie theaters, and *all* the legitimate theaters in America combined.

You can't win against the Steve Wynns.

It's something to think about.

Baccarat Comes to Las Vegas

In November 1959, the two Cellini brothers made an arrangement with the Sands Hotel in Las Vegas by which the casino would provide a roped-off area for a new table game. The casino would bankroll the game and share in its profits.

Thus did Francis "Tommy" Renzoni bring baccarat from Havana to Las Vegas. The game instantly took on the label "American baccarat" to distinguish it from *chemin de fer*.

On the first night's play, the owners of the Sands stood around, chatted, and observed. Carl Cohen smiled. Sandy Waterman maintained his usual deadpan look. And Charles Turner seemed his usual nervous self. Owners from other casinos dropped in to give the new game some courtesy play.

The players studied an instruction card that spelled out the rules, and then they began to wager.

The crew was inexperienced and tense. Sometimes the "Caller" would announce a wrong decision or direct that another card be dealt when no card was called for. Tommy would have to correct him. He did it gently. He was confident that he had a winner in this new game.

Nor was his confidence shaken when the game closed at 2 A.M., and the casino had dropped $140,000.

Years later, while chatting with Tommy in Manhattan's Gramercy Park, I asked him if the Sands' owners were upset by that first night's loss. In today's money, it would probably equal a million dollars.

"Naw," he said. "They knew my auspices."

The auspices were, of course, the Cellini brothers.

The loss wasn't all bad. Publicity about it attracted players the second evening. Here was a game that could actually be beaten. Nevertheless, the game's popularity grew at a snail's pace.

On reflection, there were reasons for its slow growth. Las Vegas was telling the world in its ads, "Come as you are!" The theme was that you could walk into any casino in your bathing suit or even in your pajamas.

By contrast, baccarat projected an elegant look. Its pit was exclusively for players. Spectators were barred, kept at a distance by velvet ropes. The game's dealers were tuxedo-clad. Its rules seemed complex.

Potential players were intimidated.

Small instruction cards were printed with the rules. "Starters" (shills) were employed to keep the game going continuously. Sometimes they would deal to each other for hours at a time, without the presence of a real player at the table.

Even today, despite the popularity of the game and its huge profits, most baccarat tables are not always full of players or going twenty-four hours.

Unlike the European versions of the game of nines, even one player was enough to get a real game started.

The action wasn't much, but when there was action, it could produce large profits for the casino.

The Las Vegas Sands was bold enough to allow $2,000 maximum wagers. This was daring at a time when $500 was the most you could bet elsewhere in the casino and that only at specially designated blackjack and craps tables.

Newcomers to the game today are surprised to learn that in those days, players helped to shuffle the cards. Also, the game was played for cash* rather than chips.

As the years sped by, stories were floated (unconfirmed) that baccarat pits were victims of armed robberies. At least that's one tale players were told when the casinos switched from playing with cash to playing with chips.

Actually, the switch was directed by the Nevada Gaming Commission. In 1973 it requested (but didn't order) the change in the belief that it would assist the casinos in cutting down on dealer embezzlement.

Counting and paying wagers with currency after each

---

*A superstition common among players then required dealers to give them their cash winnings with the green side up.

hand was a time-eating process. It is faster for a casino to shear sheep when the sheep play with chips.

More important, the more hands dealt each hour, the better for the casino. More hands meant the per had more opportunity to chew up the players.

Credit Where It's Due

America's $30-billion-a-year industry owes several markers to a fellow named Benjamin Siegel. "Bugsy," as he was never called to his face, was as handsome as a movie actor. He was certainly better looking than aging Warren Beatty, who portrayed him in a rather silly movie called *Bugsy*.

Benjamin Siegel's profession was killer-for-hire. He came from a community in Brooklyn, New York, called Brownsville where he was a boss in the Bugs-Meyer* gang. Later it became widely known as Murder, Inc.

For a sum of cash, ranging from as little as $200 to a couple of thousand dollars, Murder, Inc. would assign a member to kill anyone you didn't like. It was a well-

---

*The "Meyer" was, of course, Meyer Lansky.

thought-out business, and the organization was run with corporate efficiency.

One key to its success was that members followed orders without questioning them. Another key was that since the killer didn't know his victim, and since there was no motive or connection, law authorities faced an almost-impossible mission of tracking down the hired killer.

No one kept an exact count of the executions committed by Murder, Inc. They were said to number in the hundreds.

World War II ended in 1945, and in the autumn of that year, Benjamin Siegel drove along the road on the outskirts of a small town named Las Vegas. The road, if you stayed on it long enough, led to Los Angeles. It was a desert area off highway #91 and was considered part of Nevada's Clark County.

Suddenly he pulled the car over to the side of the isolated highway, pointed to an area, and said proudly, "This is my land." He waved his hand grandly at an expanse of dry sand, rocks, and cactus. "We're gonna build a casino on my property," he announced.

His bodyguard asked, "What property, Ben? Who'll come to this place? Camels?"

He laughed at his own joke, but stopped abruptly when his boss gave him a steel-faced look.

"I'm sorry, Ben. I—"

"Shut up!" he was told. The man shut up.

The only person who could ever kid Benjamin Siegel was the lady at his side. Her name was Virginia Hill. She dressed flamboyantly in rainbow colors. In her honor, he was to name his hotel and casino the Flamingo.

Fourteen years earlier, gambling had been legalized in Nevada. No sooner was the 1931 law passed than a licensed casino called the Northern Club opened its doors. Two others quickly followed. One, El Cortez on Fremont Street, also boasted a small hotel.

Las Vegas was a watering station for the railroad. Nothing more. Its only other attraction was a street where the merchandise was open prostitution. Beyond this and a few card rooms for poker players, it offered nothing but sand, dry heat, and desolation. Its total population was less than 20,000.

Bugsy Siegel built his casino in 1946. El Rancho Vegas had opened its doors in 1940. When that hotel and casino burned to the ground in a mysterious fire in 1960, Clark County sheriff deputies were puzzled when they found melted silver dollars in the cashier's cage, but not a scrap of burnt paper money.

Construction costs for the Flamingo quickly spiraled out of control. Tales were told of suppliers who delivered lumber in the morning and stole it back at night.

The Flamingo opened with great fanfare on December 26, 1946. Film stars from Hollywood were flown in at casino expense.

But the casino did something casinos aren't supposed to do. It consistently lost money. Odds that favor casinos continued to apply. The *per* was there, but the players weren't. People didn't come in sufficient numbers to overcome the large investment and the operating costs.

Silent partners in New York, Chicago, and points west became concerned. Not only weren't they getting a return on their investment, but Bugsy kept asking them for more working capital.

Now, "the boys" who'd put up all that money were not your usual gray-flannel-suit crowd. They had reasons for their concern. For one thing, it had not yet been established that honesty was the best policy and that honestly run table games could be more profitable than gimmicked ones with phony dice and controlled roulette wheels.

There are conflicting stories about the "how" and "why." Only the "what" is known. The investors didn't hold a formal board of directors meeting, but it was somehow decided, a few months after the Flamingo opened, that Mr. Siegel had to be replaced with someone more easily controlled.*

Murder was their business, and so it now became only a question of "where." For the sake of the city's good reputation, it had to take place out of the state. There was no other way. Not even the toughest among them had balls enough to face Siegel and tell him he was fired.

Termination took place while Siegel was lounging on the couch of Virginia Hill's mansion in Beverly Hills. The man who started his career by offering murder for a fee was gunned down by two hired killers.

The pair was so nervous that they fired more than forty shots, only nine of which penetrated Siegel's body.

---

*A man savvy about such things, but who doesn't want to be quoted, tells me that a more likely scenario is that Bugsy was killed for reasons unrelated to the casino business.

Their nervousness was justified, but for the wrong reasons.

A few days later, one of the assassins was found dead of unnatural causes in a vacant lot in North Bergen, New Jersey. The police commissioner surveyed the scene and announced to a coterie of local newsmen, "Violence has been done here."

A reporter asked, "Any theories, Commissioner?"

The commissioner thought about it. "It appears to be a suicide."

A startled reporter, having observed that the head and the body were fifteen feet apart, asked, "Commissioner, how could a man cut off his own head and walk fifteen feet?"

The commissioner ended the questioning with the profound statement, "This bears investigation."

The other member of the duo that killed Bugsy "fell or was pushed" from the roof of a six-story apartment building in the Flatbush section of Brooklyn.

Bugsy hasn't been forgotten. He and builder Del Webb were breakfasting together once when Siegel began reminiscing about some of the people he'd killed. Webb blanched. Bugsy, realizing why, offered reassurance. "Don't worry, Mr. Webb," he said. "We only kill each other."

We Only Kill Each Other became the title of a Bugsy Siegel biography by Dean Jennings (now out of print).*

---

*Some books wrongly credit Bugsy with building the second casino on the Strip. Not so. A year after El Rancho Vegas made its bow, the Last Frontier was opened for action. It was successful until the Desert

This inspired the Hilton people, who now own the Flamingo, to open a Bugsy Celebrity Theater.

Bugsy's name appears in many books about the underworld. But if the town had an ounce of sentiment, it might have erected a statue in his memory on the Las Vegas Strip. Siegel meant to Las Vegas as much as Columbus meant to America.

Francis "Tommy" Renzoni not only introduced the game to America, but was himself a baccarat degenerate. He lost personal fortune after fortune playing the very game that he introduced and supervised.

The money was plentiful. In those days, there was a large skim** divided among mobster owners and managers. It was all cash and free from tribute to that bloodsucking gang called the Internal Revenue Service. The tribute to Bugsy's former partner Meyer Lansky alone was reported to exceed $30 million.

Inn opened and dominated the Strip. After that, the Last Frontier was ill-fated. Its name was changed to New Frontier, but that didn't help.

A shabby casino named Silver Slipper was built nearby, and its owners erected a huge light-studded silver slipper that revolved on a steel shaft. As luck would have it, the revolving slipper was directly across from Howard Hughes's penthouse bedroom in the Desert Inn. Its flashing light disturbed Howard's sleep. He sent word to the owners to tone down the exuberant lights. They refused, so he bought the casino.

**The money taken from the top and not reported to tax authorities or (sometimes) to the less-powerful partner-owners.

Some casino owners weren't very discreet about hiding their riches. One of them built a mansion on his country club that featured walls that disappeared and a living room that turned around when you pushed a button. With the flick of a switch, windows became brick walls. This, while the casino man reported a small taxable income of only $20,000 a year.

Not Tommy. To Tommy, cash from the skim was for gambling. He would receive his $30,000 or $40,000 share and taxi with it to nearby Caesars Palace, where the game had just opened. He would play until he was tapioca.*

On one occasion, he was ahead $42,000 when he had a mild heart attack. He was rushed to Sunrise Hospital in a siren-screeching ambulance.

The next evening, without waiting for his cardiologist's okay, he dressed himself and taxied back to Caesars Palace. There he promptly gambled away the $42,000 he'd won plus his original $30,000 stake.

"I'm sick in the head," Tommy would tell me again and again. "I'm just plain sick in the head."

---

*An expression coined by the late colorful Manhattan saloon keeper, Toots Shor. It was the restauranteur's quaint way of saying he was "tapped out," or broke.

The Innovator

When Tommy Renzoni visited New York City, he and I would get together socially. On occasion, he would tell me his dream. He wanted to open a casino in Las Vegas that would feature only baccarat. Minimum bets would be $100. There would be a high maximum. Jackets and ties would be required of the men. And the casino would only be open from nine or ten in the evening until 3 or 4 A.M.

"Tommy," I said, "Vegas prides itself on being a twenty-four-hour town. How can you run a game that opens for only seven hours?"

He looked at me intently. "Listen, Lyle," he said, "I've been in gambling all my life. Nobody plays with my money while I'm asleep!"

Tommy never saw his dream come true. When

Howard Hughes bought the Sands at a sell-it-to-me-today-or-not-at-all bargain price, the skimming stopped. And Tommy, forced to live on his salary and a share of the tokes (tips), couldn't adjust.

He quit.

Later, at Circus Circus, he introduced a Greek game called *barbooth*. It was played in the baccarat pit at an adjoining table. It's a dead-even game. One player tosses three dice from a white cup, and another throws three from a black cup. The house take is 5 percent from the winner, giving it a healthy 2.5 percent edge.

Tommy's high hopes for the game collapsed when players found it boring. It required too many tosses of the dice to reach a decision. By contrast, baccarat is a game where the decision can be arrived at in less than a minute.

When Tommy's sweet wife died of cancer, he lost the will to live. There was income from somewhere, and he played a little baccarat. But he was listless and without direction. Sometimes he didn't answer his home phone for days at a time.

One evening, he played a few hands of baccarat at the Tropicana. But even that game no longer held his interest. When he stood up to leave, a croupier had to remind him that he'd forgotten to pick up six black ($100) chips.

He grunted acknowledgment.

He walked outside and stepped in front of a speeding car on the Strip. He was killed instantly.

They found the six black Tropicana chips in his pocket. He hadn't bothered to go to the cashier's cage to cash them.

In the years that followed, many of Tommy's crew at the Sands spread out to other hotels and became baccarat supervisors.

Today, two generations later, few of those supervising or dealing the game in casinos all over America know any of the game's history, the way it was introduced—or of the man who introduced it.

Tommy died broke. But the game he carried from Havana to Las Vegas has earned billions for casinos and will earn untold billions more before the last hand is dealt from the last baccarat shoe.

As I said earlier, there ought to be a statue somewhere in Las Vegas for Bugsy Siegel. And every baccarat pit should feature a plaque or small statue to honor Francis "Tommy" Renzoni.

Okay, enough history. Let's shuffle the cards.

Decisions, Decisions

I could assume you know the rules of baccarat. However, if there's one thing one learns in gambling, it's to take nothing for granted.

I could avoid telling you what follows for the simple reason that you don't really need to know the rules of baccarat to play baccarat. Let me repeat that: you don't need to know the rules of baccarat to play baccarat. This sets it apart from other table games.

Baccarat is often called "the game of nines." Actually it's a game of decisions, and there are only three you need make.

1. Will you bet on the next hand?
2. If your decision is to bet, will you bet on the Bank side or on the Player side?
3. How much money will you bet?

That covers it completely. *Todos*. Everything.

Let's take them one at a time. If you stand at a craps table and don't bet, it won't be long before you're asked to step aside to make way for players. At blackjack, you may occasionally indicate that you want to skip a hand. But if you simply stop betting, again you'll be asked to give up your seat. The same thing applies to all table games.

Except baccarat.

You can sit at a baccarat table, watch the game, and not bet one hand or six hands or twelve hands or half a shoe. You won't be bothered. Often, when I've just made a series of losing bets, I'll skip a few hands.

So the question "Will I bet on the next hand?" is a real one.

I'll go into how to answer the other two questions as we go along.

Today, most class casinos in Las Vegas, Reno, and Atlantic City will allow wagers starting at $25 and topping at $10,000 or more. (You can wander into a few places like Binion's Horseshoe on Fremont Street and wager $50,000 on one hand, and probably, no one will give you a second glance.)

Of course, if there's a tournament going on or a contingent of high-money players, minimums will be raised. The casino wants to get all the action it can, and so minimum bets then become $200.

Let's sit at a baccarat table and play.

A baccarat table has a crew of five. Two are seated, and their job is to collect losing bets and pay the winners.

They also keep track of the so-called "commission" on winning Bank wagers.

A "stickman" or "Caller" always stands. He or she runs the game. He observes payoffs and sometimes corrects mistakes. He also moves the game along. He announces "no more bets" and tells the player with the shoe when to deal.

At the opposite ends of the table are two supervisors. They make sure everything goes by the rules, that payoffs are accurate. They also handle credit requests.

The player sitting to your left has just dealt a hand in which the Player side won. That means the shoe is passed to you, and you've never dealt a baccarat shoe before!

Don't panic.

You will be told exactly what to do by the Caller.

You do nothing until the Caller looks at you and says, "Cards, please."

"I've never dealt before," you say.

The Caller directs you, "Draw one card from the shoe, face down, and push it toward me. Now draw one card for yourself, face down. Don't turn it over. Now deal another card, and push it toward me. Now draw a second card for yourself. Slide your two cards under the edge of your shoe, and leave them there until I ask you to turn them over."

Your two cards sit there.

In baccarat, the Player cards are always turned over first. After the Bank cards are revealed, the Banker plays to the Player total.

The two cards you dealt to the Caller will be handed,

face down, to the player who has made the largest wager on the Player side. If no one at the table has bet on the Player side, the Caller will turn them over and announce the total.

Then he or she will look at you and nod.

It's now your turn to turn over the two cards you've slid under the shoe.

You flip them over. But there are those who enjoy the dramatic tension involved in peeking at one and then the other.

When they're finally turned over and slid toward the Caller, the Caller announces their total.

Now the rules rule. The four cards you've just dealt determine whether a third card is to be dealt to the Player side or to the Bank side or to both.

If either side has a total of "8" or "9," no additional cards are dealt.

An "8" or "9" in the first two cards is called a "natural." If one side has a natural "8" and one a natural "9," the side having the "9" wins.

If both sides have "8" or both have "9," there is no victor. The hand is called a "Tie," and if you made a Tie bet, you are paid eight dollars for each dollar you wagered. (More about Ties later.) However, neither Bank nor Player bettors win or lose any money. Participants are given the opportunity to alter their bets, and the game moves on.

I won't tire you here with the other possible hands because you don't really even have to know what I've told you so far.

The Caller will tell the person with the shoe exactly

what to do: when to wait; when to draw cards; when not to draw.

There are no secrets. There are no surprises. There are no variations from the rules on that scorecard you may have for the asking.

Difficult?

I believe an educated monkey or a smart pig could be trained to play baccarat.

You're at least their equal, aren't you?

Rules & Regs

The players place their bets. When all wagers are down, no further betting is allowed.

The Caller announces, "No more bets." Then, to the player with the shoe, " Cards, please."

The person dealing from the shoe deals four cards: two for the Player side and two for the Bank side.

If you try to change your bet after the first card is out of the shoe, you'll be told gently but firmly that you can't.

As mentioned before, all cards are dealt face down. Why?

Because that's what gives baccarat its high excitement.

Consider this: since all bets must be made before any cards are dealt and since the rules of the game direct whether or not a third card will be dealt, it really wouldn't affect anything if all the cards were dealt face up.

However, this would deprive the game of its suspense. Without tension and anxiety, it wouldn't be baccarat.

As I mentioned earlier, the Player hand is slid by the Caller toward the person who has made the largest Player bet. That's the one whose task it is to show the two cards. He does so at his own pace.

That pace can sometimes give new meaning to the word "torment."

There is, for example, an Asian custom of peeking at a card slowly from each of its four sides. Then to the second card. Then back to the first. (This part I have never understood! If the peeker knows the first card is a picture card equal to zero, why is it necessary to look at it all over again?)

Finally, the two cards are pushed or tossed face up to the Caller, who places them side by side in front of him so they can be observed by all. The Caller announces the total.

Only then will the person who dealt the shoe be permitted to look at his cards. Again, this can be done as quickly as a rapid toss or as slowly as what I call "the Asian peekaboo."

(Today, almost all casino "whales" come from China and other Pacific Rim countries. Estimates of how many of these big gamblers will risk losing a million dollars on each visit, and visit Vegas two or three times yearly, range from 80 to 200.)

In any case, these two cards are placed side by side by the Caller parallel to the two Player cards.

The Caller announces whether a third card is to be dealt to the Player hand, the Bank hand, both hands, or neither hand.

How it works is that the two cards in each hand are added together. All 10s and picture cards count as 10. *Since 9 is the highest possible hand one can hold, the digit on the left cancels itself out.*

Let me explain how this works. You have two 8s. That's 16. But the digit on the left is canceled, so your total is 6.

Thus two pictures equal 20. Cancel the 2, and you have 0. *Nada*. Nothing.

A 9 and an 8 equal 17. Cancel the left digit, and you have 7.

A picture and a 4 equal 14. Cancel the left digit, and you have 4.

A 5 and a 6 add up to 11. You have 1.

A 6 and 6 equal 12. You have 2.

Do you begin to get the picture? Good!

Suits have no meaning. Diamonds, clubs, hearts, and spades are all equal citizens in the nation of nines.

Except for an occasional wisecracking jackass at the far end of the table, there are no jokers in this game.

Let's move down the ladder.

If either side has a total of 7, that hand does not receive a third card. The side with the 7 stands.

If Player's hand totals 6, it too stands and does not receive a third card.

The balance of the rules may appear complicated to newcomers. They aren't.

If neither side has that natural 8 or 9, and the two

Player cards add up to 0, 1, 2, 3, 4, or 5, the Player is dealt a third card.

Now, stick with me closely. This is the part that confounds novices.

It is the value of the third card dealt to the Player *and not the total of the three Player cards* (as wrongly reported in those amateur books on the subject) that determines whether the Bank side will draw a card for itself.

1. Except, of course, where the Player's first two cards total 8 or 9, the Bank almost always draws a third card. If the Bank's two cards total 3, and it deals the Player an 8, Bank doesn't draw. It does draw a card if dealing any card to the Player but an 8.

2. If the Bank's two cards add up to 4, and it deals a 1, 8, 9, or 10 to the Player hand, it doesn't draw. It draws if dealing any other card.

3. If the Bank's two cards total 5, and it deals a 1, 2, 3, 8, 9, or 10, the Bank doesn't draw a third card. The Bank does draw for itself if it deals any other denomination card.

4. If the Bank's two-card total is 6, and it deals Player a 1, 2, 3, 4, 5, 8, 9, or 10 as its third card, the Bank doesn't draw a card for itself. Bank draws only if it deals the Player a 6 or 7.

5. If the Bank has a 7, it stands, no matter which third card it deals to Player.

Opposite is the way a casino lays out the rules on their instruction cards. Basically, they're the same thing.

The beginning player is sometimes startled by some

RULES: PLAYER

When Player's first two cards total:	0-1-2-3-4-5	Draws a card
	6-7	Stands
	8-9	Natural-Neither hand draws

RULES: BANKER

When the PLAYER stands on 6 or 7, the BANKER will always draw on totals of 0-1-2-3-4 and 5, and stand on 6-7-8 and 9.

When the PLAYER does not have a natural, the BANKER shall draw on the totals of 0-1 or 2, and then observe the following rules:

When Banker's first two cards total:	Draws when Player's third card is:	Does not draw when Player's third card is:
3	1-2-3-4-5-6-7-9-10	8
4	2-3-4-5-6-7	1-8-9-10
5	4-5-6-7	1-2-3-8-9-10
6	6-7	1-2-3-4-5-8-9-10
7	STANDS	
8-9	NATURAL-NEITHER HAND DRAWS	

If the PLAYER takes no third card BANKER stands on 6.
The hand closest to 9 wins.
All winning bets are paid even money.
Winning BANK bets are charged 5 percent commission.
TIE bets pay 8 to 1.

Rule cards.

situations. For example, let's say both Bank and Player have totals of 4. Player is dealt an ace (1). The game is over. Player wins 5 to 4.

How come?

Look again. The Bank, having a 4, does not draw when giving Player a 1, 8, 9, or 10.

It is difficult for the inexperienced player to understand why, when both sides start with the same total of 4, the Bank isn't given a third card and a chance to equal or beat the Player. Those are the rules, baby. That's the way it is.

Another instance that puzzles newcomers happens when the Bank's two-card total is 6. The Player's two-card total is 0. *Baccara.* Nothing. Player is dealt a third card, and it's a 6. A Tie? Nope. You must remember that Bank having 6, and dealing a 6 or 7 to the Player as Player's third card, *must* draw a third card, too. This, no matter what the Player's final total may be after the 6 is dealt.

The odds are against the Bank on this one. Of the 416 cards in the eight-deck shoe, 128 are picture cards and 10s and won't affect anything. Only one of the 96 aces, deuces, and treys will help. Every other one of the 192 cards will bust the 6 to a lower total.

Is your head spinning?

Too much information to digest all at once?

Relax.

You need not know any of this. There are people who've played baccarat for years and don't know the elementary items I've just spelled out.

The Caller controls the game. The players have no need to know or understand the rules. They don't have to speak English. In fact, they don't have to speak at all!

In addition to directing the dealing and calling the totals, the Caller watches, along with the supervisors, as bets on losing sides are collected and bets on winning sides are paid.

Not to worry about the Caller cheating. He's an employee. As a member of the baccarat team, he shares in the tokes (tips). He can get rich on tips, but he ain't ever gonna get rich on his casino salary.

In addition to the two supervisors who observe everything from their ends of the table, there is a hidden camera watching from the ceiling that is recording every move. If there is a serious dispute, management needs only to replay the disputed hand on film. These cameras are so sophisticated that they can zoom in to show the beads of sweat on your forehead. Superimposed on each frame of the film is the date and time of the action—down to seconds.

Does this eliminate all error?

Hardly.

Wrong calls are made occasionally, but they're quickly corrected.

As often as not, the wrong calls favor the customers.*

---

*I once played at a table in Atlantic City where a hand was a 6-6 tie and a tie bettor was paid off. On the next hand, the Player had 4 and the Bank 6. The Player's third card was 3, making a total of 7. The Bank's third card was a picture, making a total of 6. The lady Caller erroneously announced, "Six, six. Pay the tie bet." A half dozen other players, some betting on Bank and some on Player, sat mesmerized.

Wrong payoffs are made, and these, too, are quickly corrected.

Incidentally, the person dealing from the shoe continues to deal from the shoe as long as he or she deals hands on which the Bank side wins or which are Ties. As soon as a Player side wins, the shoe passes to the player on the right.

A winning hand is a "pass," and winning is "making a pass."

No one can be forced to take the shoe. The player may pass it on to the next person on his right without dealing or even after dealing a hand or two.

A point to remember: the fact that you are dealing the shoe does not require you to bet on the Bank side. You can "bet against yourself" by betting Player. This is unusual enough so that the Caller, on seeing this, will say for all to hear, "Dealer is on the Player side."

This is important, and I'll refer to it several times in this book for reasons you'll soon know.

To repeat: when you hold the shoe it is perfectly okay to bet on Player side.

Often it's the wisest thing to do.

When I discuss my now-famous "Rule of Three," you'll better understand why.

Nobody corrected her. The tie bet was paid and the cards dropped into the discard slot.

I couldn't believe that I had seen what I had seen. It had all happened in less than a minute.

A man who'd been paid for a second consecutive tie win glanced my way, and knew from the expression on my face that I had seen the error. He winked and shrugged. He certainly wasn't going to object.

The Game Begins

The modern baccarat table has fourteen seats for players. (The original tables seated only twelve.) On the
green-felt-covered table in front of each chair is a
numeral to identify the player. These numerals range
from #1 to #15.* Thus, seven players can be accom-
modated on each side of the table.

---

*If you think they can't total seven and seven as four-
teen, and #15 would indicate fifteen seats, keep in
mind that factor called "player superstition." There is
no seat #13. If there was a #13, it's doubtful many
players would sit there. The irrational fear of "13" is
called "triskaidekaphobia."
Not all tables are covered with green felt. One Hong
Kong contingent flew to Las Vegas and insisted that
the color be changed to red, the Chinese lucky color.

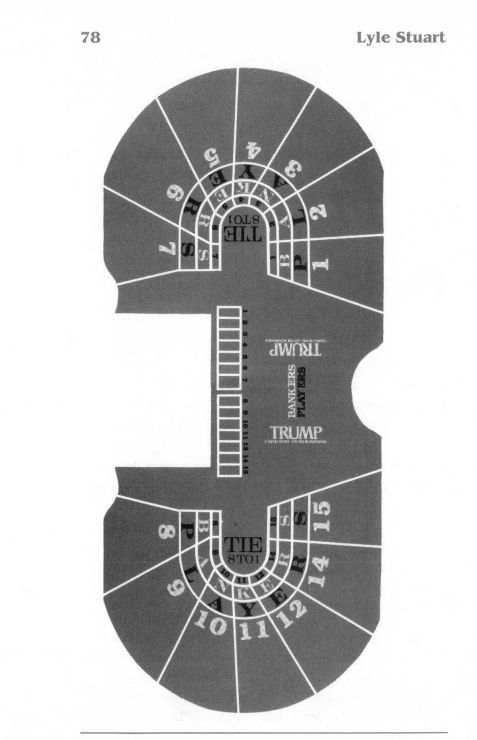

The shape of a baccarat table.

The game is directed from the center of the table. Two croupiers sit there. Each has a clear view of the seven players on his or her side.

Facing the two, also in the center of the table but on the opposite side, and located in the kidney-shaped indenture, is the Caller. The Caller doesn't sit. He or she always stands.

The Caller directs the game. Callers must see that the proper number of cards are dealt, that no bets are made after the first card is dealt, and that the croupiers (dealers) first collect all losing wagers and then pay the winners exactly what is due them.

Like the stickman at a craps table, the Caller is also a promoter. One is bombarded with a constant line of chatter encouraging players to "bet the Tie"—the most profitable bet on the table for the casino. The casino advantage on this bet is 14.40 percent.

As mentioned earlier, each table has two supervisors. They watch to make sure cards are thoroughly mixed. They make sure that bets are paid properly. They stand at opposite ends of the table and are called *laddermen*.

It was. So was the carpet in the pit and the cloth fabric that covered the chairs. Even the female shills were told to wear red dresses only.

Asians seem, but probably aren't, more superstitious than other groups. If a big-money player leaves his seat for an hour or two for dinner, no other player is allowed to sit in the empty chair or even stand in front of it to make a bet. If that understanding is violated, the original player will quit, believing that another person has stolen or changed his luck.

The name originates from European roulette where a supervisor sits on a high chair and, to get to his seat, must climb a small ladder.

When table action involves large sums of money, the pit boss, the shift boss, and even the casino manager will sometimes appear at the table standing and observing unobtrusively.

I once dealt twenty-two consecutive winning Bank hands at Caesars Palace. It is not only my personal record for winning passes, but the largest number of passes I've ever seen made by anyone. By the time I'd made fifteen of these passes, there were more casino executives watching my deal than there were players sitting at the table.

Baccarat is played with eight decks. Often players will leave the table at the end of the shoe. If a nearby table is in action, and seats are available, they'll move there.

Or they'll take their chips and walk.

This being the case, in the past, casinos have experimented with using additional decks in the shoe. The theory was that this would keep players at the table longer. The ploy didn't work.

An exception can be found on Fremont Street in downtown Las Vegas where the El Cortez casino uses only a seven-deck shoe.

A casino near the railroad once boasted "the largest baccarat shoe in history." That shoe was a long plastic arm that contained 144 decks of cards. It didn't work. It was an attention-getting novelty, but players were uncomfortable with it and kept away. It was eventually discontinued.

When the table opens, eight fresh decks of cards are unwrapped. Jokers are removed, and the eight decks are spread out, face up and in sequence so that both the dealers and the players can look at the cards and make sure all is in order.

In Las Vegas, the odds are that they'll unwrap Bee brand cards made by the US Playing Card Company. This century-old card is the only one that contains a high rag content. This gives it what casino owners call "a good memory" because it snaps back into position after being bent.

In Atlantic City, it's more likely that Gemaco brand cards will be used because they have strong resistance to the city's high humidity.

The decks are shuffled, one or two at a time, and then mixed into the other decks. When the eight decks have been combined, each of the two dealers are given approximately half of the eight decks to mix again. After much shuffling, all 416 cards are merged into one pack.

Then another ritual is followed, though not as universally as it used to be. The cards are "laced" or "salted." That is, a stack of forty or fifty cards is taken from the top and starting at the front, cards are dropped rapidly and randomly into the decks. This is supposed to guarantee that the cards are not "fixed"—for each card dropped in randomly changes the entire sequence of the cards that follow.

A blank yellow or white plastic card is used as an indicator. When the shuffle and lacing have been completed, the dealer offers the indicator card to a player. With his other hand, he holds the eight decks together.

The player inserts the card into the decks. House rules usually prescribe that the player's cut must be further than one deck's thickness on either the front or the back of the eight decks. The cards are then divided by the cut so that the stack in back of the indicator card is moved to the front of it.

The cut decides how the seventy-two to seventy-eight hands in the average shoe will be dealt. The die is cast. Nothing can change it. The number of hands that will be Bank winners or Player winners has been ordained by that cut. What remains is your decision on whether to bet Bank or Player on any given hand.

Next, a line of cards from the back of the deck is spread out, face down. The croupier counts and inserts another yellow or black indicator card in front of the fourteenth card. These fourteen cards are placed in back of the deck with the indicator card in front of them.

When this indicator card appears, more than seventy hands later, the Caller announces, "The next hand will be the last hand of the shoe."

The eight decks are placed in the shoe, and a transparent cover is placed over the top, locking in the cards.

The dealer draws the first card and turns it face up. This card directs how many cards are to be "burned"— drawn, turned face up, and dropped into the discard slot. They fall into the large bucket that hangs underneath the table.

For example, if the first card is a 6, six cards will be "burned" (discarded). If the first card is a 10 or a picture, ten cards are "burned."

There is an Asian superstition that if the first card is a high one, the shoe will be a Bank shoe. If it is a low one, it will favor the Player side. I've rarely observed cards live up to that superstition. When they do, it is, of course, coincidence.

Players, not dealers, deal the cards.

"Place your bets," the Caller says. "Baccarat is about to begin."

The shoe is moved to the person sitting in seat #1. That person will deal the first hand. But nothing happens until the Caller is satisfied that all bets are down.

"Cards, please," the Caller says.

The game has begun.

The Rule of
Three

When I explained my Rule of Three in the pages of my original book on casino gambling, I wrote that it could be worth hundreds of times the cost of the book to those who adopted it.

In Irving Berlin's *Cheek to Cheek*, a song written for the 1935 Fred Astaire-Ginger Rogers movie, *Top Hat*, there is a lyric line that refers to "a gambler's lucky streak."

There *are* lucky streaks. There will be times in your casino forays when you can do no wrong. Almost everything you touch will turn winner.

There are also unlucky streaks. These are more likely the norm. During these times, you won't be able to win a bet to save your backside.

I said in my first book that there are no systems, but

B	P	B	P	B	P	B	P
	1	10		(21)		28	
	(2)	11			17	29	
	3	12		22		(30)	
	4	—		23		31	
	5		10		18	—	
1		13			19	—	
(2)		14			(20)		26
—		15			21	32	27
3			11	24			27
4			12	—		(33)	
	6	16		—			28 29
—		—		—		(34)	30
	7	17		25			30
5			13	—		35 36	
6			14	26			31 32
	8	(18)			22	37	
7		19			(23)	—	33
8		(20)			24	38	34
	9		15	(27)		—	
9		(16)			25		

that casino games could be beaten *for a short time only* through a combination of disciplines and philosophies.

My Rule of Three will protect you from yourself. It's a powerful steel gate that will avoid those disastrous losses that all too often are prompted by your own stubbornness.

Time and again, I have watched players so emotionally involved in stubbornly bucking a streak that money no longer seemed to be money as they went through their entire bankrolls in one sitting.

I used to do it myself.

Professional gambler Louis Holloway demonstrated for me the error of my ways. He was, incidentally, the only person I ever knew who made a living from gaming on the player's side. (He wrote the excellent book *Full-Time Gambler*, which I published, but which is now out of print.)

The Rule of Three says that if a thing happens three times in a row, *you either bet on the streak, or you don't bet at all*.

Let's use baccarat as an example. The Bank side has won three times in a row. Which side do you bet on now?

———

This is a normal. There were no sensational streaks, but I was lucky in my guesswork and disciplined enough so when I didn't have a strong guess-instinct, I'd skip the hand. I played sixty of the seventy-two hands in which there were decisions. I won thirty-one of these and lost twenty-nine. The shoe was Tie-packed in that twelve Ties were dealt.

We know that Bank and Player have almost equal chances to come up, not unlike heads or tails in a coin toss.

You can say, "Bank has come up three times, so now is the time to bet Player."

You *could* be right.

Now suppose the Bank side wins again. That makes four in a row.

Now you're *sure* Player will come up, so you bet it again.

Suicide.

Under my rule, *you go with the flow or you don't go.* If red comes up three times at roulette, you bet red or you don't bet.

If three hands at dice are losers, you bet the Don't Pass" line or you don't bet.

If Bank has won three hands in a row in baccarat, you bet Bank or you don't bet.

Sure, Player will often come up in this situation. But that isn't the point. If you follow my rule, you'll avoid being sucked into a financially disastrous quagmire. That *is* the point.

♠ ♦ ♥ ♣

The scene was the baccarat table at the Las Vegas Sands. My wife Carole and I were passing time because Tony Pepe had someone in his barber's chair, two more customers were waiting, and I wanted one of his marvelous haircuts. (Adnan Khashoggi, then one of the world's wealthiest men, once flew Tony to New York City just so he could have a Pepe-styled morning hair trim!)

In those days, the Sands had the not-very-bright rule that if your wagers were less than $500, your maximum bet was $2,000, whereas if you bet nothing less than $500 each hand, you could bet as much as $4,000 a hand.

Their convoluted explanation was that they didn't want someone sitting down with $20, getting lucky, and then working up to $4,000 bets "with our money."

The chips were in the player's possession, but they still considered it "their money." This is much like the player who loses and then talks about the casino having *his* money.

If the money is in your hands, it's *your* money. If it's in their hands, it's *their* money. Even if you've carefully hand printed your name on the face of every bill!

The Sands' rule made no sense to me.

What difference is it if a $4,000 wager is made by the player in seat #6 or the player in seat #5? If the guy in seat #5 now bets $4,000, the odds against him are exactly the same as they are against the man in seat #4.

There was a second explanation. "We don't want somebody doubling up." This double-up strategy takes advantage of the stretch between the lowest bet and the highest bet. Thus if you start with $20 and lose, you bet $40. If you lose, you bet $80,

then $160,
then $320,
then $640,
then $1,280.

Bang! With your next wager, you're head-on bucking the $2,000 maximum. If the Bank wins seven in a row, you're out $2,540 in your quest to win twenty bucks.

True, seven in a row doesn't happen very often.

But it does happen.

So I sat and watched the fellow across from me do just that. He bet $20 on the Player side. Then $40. Then $80. He usually won by the third or fourth sequence. Twenty-dollar chips were piled chin-high in front of him.

The shoe passed to someone at the opposite end of the table.

I bet Player and lost. I sat out the next two Player wins.

Now my choice was to either bet Player or not bet at all.

I bet Bank.

The man with the shoe dealt fourteen more Banks! His fifteen consecutive Bank wins were the most I'd witnessed in months. (I mentioned earlier my own string of twenty-two passes.)

Long before it was over, the man across from me had lost all his chips.

And when it was over, I nodded to him sympathetically. At which point, he said sadly, "Want to hear an irony? The fellow who just made those fifteen passes is my boss!"

The Rule of Three isn't difficult to understand. And yet I've been perplexed by players who sit and bet on Bank as if they're mesmerized while the shoe moves

---→

This shoe had a lovely run of 15 Bank hands. It was also the shoe that knocked out that fellow who was doing the doubling-up routine.

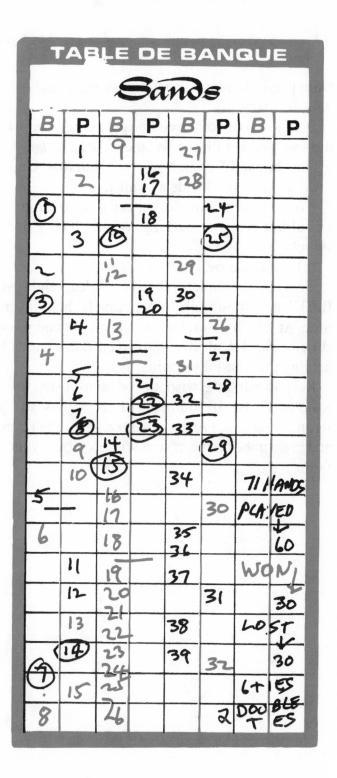

from player to player, chalking up eight and ten Player wins in a row.

I sat next to an otherwise bright young man who held the shoe and bet Player. In other words, he was "betting against himself." Nothing wrong with that. On his first deal, he dealt Bank side a winner.

After this scenario was repeated for the fourth time, I couldn't resist remarking to him, "Why don't you switch?"

"One more time," he said.

He one-more-timed-it until he'd dealt eight winning Bank hands to himself, except that he bet Player every time. At which point, he was tapped out and passed the shoe to me. I dealt two additional Bank hands before dealing the first Player win.

Keep in mind the wisdom and built-in stop loss of the Rule of Three. If you bet with the streak and you're wrong, *you lose only one wager*. If you bet against it and are stubborn, the casino will soon own your potato farm.

Money Management

People sometimes ask what I consider the ideal situation at the baccarat table. Obviously, it would be to win every hand.

This ain't gonna happen, Mister.

No way, Gwendolyn.

So I aim for the next best target. This one exists in reality; the other, in your dreams. I'm satisfied to win one and lose one if, in doing so, *I win more money than I lose*.

Since the odds against you are less than 1.25 percent on either Player or Bank bets, you have almost a 50-50 chance of winning your wager.

These are the rules I follow:

1) When possible (even if it means standing around for half an hour), I enter the game when a new shoe is about to be dealt.

2) I try to stick to my Rule of Three.

P	B	P	B	P	B	P	B
1			12	18		31	
2		10			26		33
	1	11			27	32	
	2	12		19		(33)	
	3		13	20			(34)
3		(13)		21			35
	4	14		22		34	
4			14	23		(35)	
5			(15)		28	(36)	
	5		16		29	~	
	6		17	24			
	→		—	25			
6			18	26			
—			19		(30)		
	7		20	~			
	8		21	—			
7		15		27			
	9		(22)	28			
	10		23		31		
(8)			24	29			
—			25	30			
				—			
	11	16					
9		(17)			32		

Let's say that I've decided which side I'm going to bet on. Let's say I bet eight chips.*

I win. I now have sixteen chips.

I collect the eight that I've won and remove four from my original wager, thus cutting the bet in half.

If I lose the next bet, I'm fulfilling the game average of 50-50. *But I've won money.*

Like that wonderful song-lyric writer, Ira Gershwin, I tend to favor the Player side, although I'm not as rigid as he was about it. But I do tend to play Player as the shoe moves around. When it comes to me, I usually switch to the Bank side.

If I win my second bet, I have won twelve chips. I retain seven and bet five.

---

*I happen to be talking about $8,000, but Hank Greenspun, the late publisher of the *Las Vegas Sun*, noted in his critique of my first book that by talking these large amounts, I remove the reality from readers who play $2, $5, or $10. I don't agree, but on this occasion, I'll defer to him for simplicity's sake.

Although the final score in this shoe was Player's 36 to Bank's 35, there were a couple of nice streaks in this one.

There was a streak of eight Bank wins. Then, after a single Player win, there were four more for the Bank.

I played sixty-one of the seventy-one decision hands dealt. I won thirty-three of these, thanks largely to that Bank streak. I lost twenty-eight.

There were eight Ties, one of them a Tie-after-Tie.

If I win the third bet, I have now won seventeen. I prudently remove three more chips.

Now I bet seven. If I win the next bet, I subtract four or five.

I'm on a streak. But unlike players who increase their bets with their winnings and never expect to lose, I know that every rainbow has a beginning and an end. So, when I lose a bet, *I've made certain to have won money on every hand but the last.*

If I get a feeling that I'm experiencing one of those rare "miracle" streaks, my wagers soon climb to the maximum allowed. Then I really rake it in! I'm not Kerry Packer with his $25,000 and $100,000 chips and his $250,000 wagers, but I have bet as much as $12,000 on a hand—and won!

That's one approach.

There's another. She's the offspring of Lady Impatience.

If I'm "nice money" ahead for my visit, I'll make the eight-unit maximum bet, and if I win, collect the eight and reduce my bet by one chip, making the next bet seven. If I win that one, it's maximum all the way. This is obviously a more radical approach than the first. And here is where Dame Circumstance does her little pirouette.

When she shows her pretty face, just hope that her pretty legs will hold up for another few dances. And if you win a few, look up at the casino chandelier and say to it, "No, I'm not going to try to take you home with me today."

Rise up, and go directly to the cashier's cage to cash in your chips. Then, run, do not walk, from the casino.

Don't look back!

Recipe for Success

There are several ingredients that make for a winning gaming session. These are, in my order of importance:

1. Money management.
2. Being lucky.
3. Knowing when to leave.

Let's tackle them in reverse order. But first here is forty-one cents' worth of philosophy.

Nobody is permanently lucky. We all end up as minerals that feed the plants and flowers. The grass is victorious, even over casino owners.

Author Mario Puzo titled his Las Vegas novel *Fools Die*, but we're all fools and we all die. Not in the entire history of the human race with its billions of individuals has a single human escaped dying.

Erich Maria Remarque wrote *All Quiet on the Western Front*. He said it well in his *Shadows in Paradise* where he wrote about ". . . the sadness we all feel because everything passes, and man is the only animal who knows it."

Humans are conscious of death and because most people can't face it, they die, as Yeats said, many times. And during their lifetimes, they engage in monkeylike antics, praying to gods and supporting palaces for the modern-day witch doctors (call them ministers, priests, or rabbis) in what has to be the most profitable legalized racket on earth today.*

I best like philosopher Bertrand Russell's appraisal of the superstitions, myths, compulsions, and obsessions we call religions. He said, "My own view of religion is that of Lucretius. I regard it as a disease born of fear and as a source of untold misery to the human race."

Amen!

The element of risk is an element of life. Chance, fear, hope, and greed are motivators of human conduct and have been since the first human animal got off all fours by standing upright.

I sometimes am critical of those who seem to take no risks at all in life. But they're not my favorite people.

---

*The skimming that took place by the mob of Las Vegas casinos in the heyday of the tough guy was nothing as compared to the hundreds of millions that were swindled some years back from the Vatican by its pious financial managers.

You know the type. They don't gamble at all. They carefully save their nickels, dimes, and dollars for a rainy day or a reckoning with retirement. They, too, are gamblers, for they are betting on a future time that they may never live to see.

So, Dear Reader, enjoy life while you may, and enjoy it particularly when you have been lucky. In casino terms, being in the right place at the right time and handling your money the right way makes for a winning combination.

Is the shoe streaking for Player? Is it streaking for Bank? Is it playing "chop-chop"—hip-hopping from one side to the other?

There is no such thing as a "lucky table" because the cards tell one story and your wagers tell the more important one.

You have your opportunity to play it any way you wish. Every bet that you lose could have been a winner if placed differently. And, conversely, every bet you won could have been a loser.

When it's over, and you get up from the table and have more money than you sat down with, you say you've been "lucky."

As I mentioned earlier, it isn't always necessary to win more *bets* than you lose. It *is* necessary to win more *money* than you lose. Luck helps, but it isn't always necessary.

A man named Major Riddle, who was a major owner of the Dunes Hotel in Las Vegas that was razed in 1996, used to pontificate that the way to beat baccarat was to "follow the shoe." Did Player win the last wager? Then you bet Player and continue to bet Player until Bank wins. Then you bet Bank. And so forth.

It certainly insures that you'll catch streaks.

It doesn't insure that you'll win.

What will insure that you win is:

1) A clear plan or strategy mapped out *before* you enter the baccarat pit on how long you'll play and how much you'll gamble with.
2) Getting up and walking away when you're a winner.
3) Leaving town a winner. Even if you're only a few dollars ahead, get on that plane a winner!

It's a simple prescription, isn't it?

Well, you could choke on the number of letters I've had from readers of my first book who reported that they followed my advice and won $1,500 or $2,500 or $6,000, but then stayed around too long and lost all of it back.

We all have idiosyncrasies. And most of us are superstitious. It's almost impossible to approach the gaming table without being superstitious. Even I hear myself calling, "Same dice, please!" when one of the cubes bounces from the table to the floor.

Would it matter if a different cube was substituted? Aren't they all made identical to the 10,000th of an inch?

My own philosophy is that it is better to never have won than to have won and pissed it all away by lingering too long at the tables.

If you're fortunate enough to accumulate winnings, think of yourself as a highwayman who just robbed a stagecoach. The sheriff and his deputies are coming 'round the bend to gun you down if you stick around.

You'd know what to do then, wouldn't you?

You'd gallop away as fast as your horse's hooves could move.

Do it.

The Commission Thing

When you make a Player bet at baccarat and you win, the house pays you dollar for dollar. Bet twenty dollars and win and they give you twenty more.

On winning Bank bets, they seem to pay you dollar for dollar, but then they rack up 5 percent of the amount of your wager in a box in front of the croupier that has the same number as the number of your seat.

They call it "commission."

It isn't, really.

What happens is that because of the structure of the rules, Bank side will win 50.68 percent and Player side wins 49.32 percent of all decisions. (Tie bets are "no decision.")

Including Ties, Player side has a 44.62 percent probability of winning, a 45.85 percent probability of losing, and a 9.53 percent probability of a Tie.

The true percentage against betting the Bank side is (.95 X 45.85) ($1.00 X 44.62) = 1.06 percent. Thus the odds against Bank bets is 1.06 percent and against Player bets, 1.23 percent.

The house wagers even money against your Player bets. However, the Bank side has the probability of winning more hands than Player in each shoe. To assure the house its vigorish (or profit), the house wagers only ninety-five cents to your dollar on the Bank side.

By doing this, they set the Bank odds against you. Otherwise, if the Bank bets paid the same even money that Player bets pay, the advantage would be very much with the Bank.

There isn't much difference between those percentages over a short period of time. But the illusion remains that because Bank does win more hands in each average shoe, it is smarter to bet Bank.

To restate it in a slightly different way, a baccarat shoe will give the Bank side a winning average of 46 percent of all hands and the Player side a winning average of 44.6 percent of all hands. The remaining hands end up as Ties.

By paying ninety-five cents to a dollar on winning Bank hands, the casino will earn 1.06 percent profit on Bank hands and 1.23 percent profit on Player hands.

Baccarat would be played at a funereal pace if the house had to pay you ninety-five cents for each winning dollar in your Bank box. Thus grew the practice of the dealers keeping score with colored markers in a little square in front of them that has your seat number.

If the dealer doesn't know you, he may point out

what you owe from time to time and invite you to settle.

If you're a regular, they usually won't bother you until the shoe has been played out. At this point, all "commissions" are collected from the players.

I hate surprises, such as being told I owe lots of "commission." So I keep my eye on the little brown markers (each representing $100 worth of obligation) and, from time to time, toss chips to the dealer with the instruction, "Browns down."

Unlike people who are rigid Player bettors because, psychologically, they "hate to pay the commission," I love to take browns down because they represent winning wagers.

It may be worth noting that both in Las Vegas and in Atlantic City, one can invariably find a casino that, for competitive reasons, offers the game with the commission reduced to 4 percent. At this writing, the 4 percent is available at the Atlantic City Hilton.

Winning. Running away. Those are the elements. That's what baccarat is all about.

If you sit too long in that comfortable seat, that seat could become your financial coffin.

The System Sickness

A system to beat baccarat?

Many have tried. *All* have failed.

I know an art dealer who put aside his Dalis, Picassos, and Portocarreros so he could devote his days and nights analyzing full-shoe scorecards on his computer. At last, he believed he had devised a system that could beat the house. It was convoluted, but after certain patterns emerged, you did thus-and-so, etc.

He flew from New York to Las Vegas to test it. He had $6,000 in his pocket. He flew home the next day with $67. There was a flaw in the system.

A similar sad scenario is repeated dozens of times each week. Same plot, different players.

A fellow named Henry J. Tamburin ran a blackjack school and conducted seminars on gaming. In the spring of 1983, he collaborated with a writer of gambling books named Dick Rahm to produce a baccarat "system."

The pair claimed to have played 175 million games of baccarat on their computers. They reportedly gained insights from the results that enabled them to devise a card-counting system. This system, they said, gives the baccarat player an advantage over the casino.

Tamburin was kind enough to send me a copy of the book. Tamburin had a Ph.D. after his name, and Rahm had an M.S. after his. They had the credentials, but, alas, their concept failed to upset baccarat the way the findings of Edward Thorp and Larry Revere's upset blackjack.

The book contains many charts and tables. One of these explains why the rules were designed so that Bank draws a card with a total of 3 when dealing a 9 as Player's third card.

The Player side receives a third card only if it has a total of 0, 1, 2, 3, 4, 5. An additional 9 will therefore give Player one of the following totals: 9, 0, 1, 2, 3, 4.

Now, since Bank has only a total of three, if no card were drawn by the Bank, the Player would win hands totaling 9 or 4, tie with 3, and lose with 0, 1, or 2.

This, say the authors of *Winning Baccarat Strategies*, gives the Bank the edge of 3-to-2. But if Bank draws to its 3, you then open the following possibilities:

$$3 + 0 = 3$$
$$3 + 1 = 4$$
$$3 + 2 = 5$$
$$3 + 3 = 6$$

$$3 + 4 = 7$$
$$3 + 5 = 8$$
$$3 + 6 = 9$$
$$3 + 7 = 10$$
$$3 + 8 = 1$$
$$3 + 9 = 2$$

Thus, the Bank has a 3-to-2 chance of improving its hand. And, by drawing that third card, it increases its advantage over the Player hand to 44-25.

The book also offers three counting systems. Despite the interesting technical information and the mathematical breakdown of the value of individual cards and expectations, I tend to doubt very much that a player can prosper by doing all that record keeping, just to manufacture an occasional possible clue that the balance of the shoe could favor Bank side or could favor Player side.

Here's another case. A man contacted me who truly believed he had discovered a pattern in random hands.

He tossed thousands of pennies. Although the probability of heads or tails is identical for each toss of the coin and without regard to any previous tosses, he was convinced that he'd uncovered a definite pattern in random patterns.

Applied to baccarat, he felt it could give the player a consistent edge over the house.

The problem was that it required lots of hindsight.

The Gamblers Book Club* offers books that chronicle

---

*Don't go to Las Vegas without visiting their shop.

as many as 25,000 decisions generated randomly with a computer. One such booklet reported that Bank won 11,494 of the hands, or 45.976 percent of the time against its probability win of 45.842 percent. Player won 11,111 hands or 44.448 percent of the time as against a probability win of 44.683 percent. This means that the deviation was less then $1/4$-of-1 percent from the probability expectancy. Small wonder that casino operators who understand probability can sleep peacefully at night.

To sum up, I have yet to see any way for card-counters to defeat the game of baccarat with a card-counting system.

Luck can do it.

Winning-and-running can do it.

Money management can most certainly do it.

But not counting cards.

Many players have tried to convince me that otherwise is the case. I was told about a man who lazed about in casinos in the Caribbean and stumbled onto a method of counting cards that would give him a clue as to when Ties were most probable.

According to the story, he eventually migrated to Las Vegas. He allegedly (to fool the tax collector) became an encyclopedia salesman. Occasionally he buys a set of encyclopedias for himself just to maintain the facade.

You'll find it at 630 South 11th Street, Las Vegas, NV 89101. It has the world's most complete collection of books, magazines, and pamphlets on gambling. The prices are surprisingly reasonable, too. Or, send them a stamped, self-addressed envelope for their current catalog.

(His basement must be crowded with encyclopedias!)

He visits casinos and plays baccarat for small stakes. When the count is right, he makes graduated bets on Tie until he wins—$25, $50, $75, $100, etc.

He varies his play from casino to casino so that he is known as a modest player and an affable fellow.

He is careful not to draw attention to himself.

It is said he was nearly broke when he arrived at McCarran Airport. Now he is said to live in a house that cost him $300,000 (fully paid, no mortgage) and is said to be rolling in money.

Grimm's isn't the only place you find fairy tales. Las Vegas produces its fair share. I believe this is one. Although I promised the source of this story complete confidentiality, I was never able to secure (1) a name, (2) an address, or even (3) a physical description of the man who makes it on Ties.

Nor are there that many encyclopedia salesmen in Las Vegas.

The only way to guarantee profits at the game of baccarat is to be on the casino's side. In other words, be an owner.

Otherwise, if you sit at a table long enough, their shoe is going to take your shoes. Just make certain it doesn't take your shirt and shorts, too!

Cheating

Years ago, I was relaxing in the backyard of the Las
Vegas home of the pit boss of one of the top baccarat
games in town.

A full-sized baccarat table stood on the grass turf
next to his heated swimming pool. He was teaching his
son to deal and to supervise the game.

We had just discussed whether it would be easier for
a customer to cheat at a nearly empty table or a full one.
I remarked that when there were many people around,
there were many pairs of eyes and more chances that a
cheat would be caught.

My host insisted that the opposite was true: the more
people at a table, the less attention the individual player
receives, and the easier it would be for him to cheat.

The talk about cheating turned to a Fremont Street

sawdust joint that had been padlocked by the Nevada Gaming Board after its agents discovered that the casino had removed certain ten-point cards and aces from its blackjack shoes to improve the house odds against the customers.

"Except for those gimmicked shoes with their hidden reflectors, where the dealer can see the next card to be dealt, so he can signal it to a confederate who is playing at the table, I've heard that there isn't much chance of cheating or being cheated at the baccarat table," I said.

While we chatted, the pit boss shuffled the cards, seemingly in an aimless fashion. "You're an old newspaper reporter," he said. "Weren't you taught to believe nothing you hear and only half of what you see?"

I laughed. "No. I was taught to get it first, but to first get it right."

"Cheating comes with the territory," he went on. "There isn't a casino in the world that doesn't spend big dollars policing both the dealers and the players."

My friend slid the plastic cover on top of the shoe and began to deal hands.

"Do you think I'm cheating now?" he asked.

"Not that I can notice," I replied.

"The next nine hands will all be Bank winners."

He proceeded to deal nine hands. The Bank won every hand. Nor were these obvious wins like "naturals." Sometimes the score began Player 3 and Bank 2 and ended up Bank 7 and Player 6.

I was impressed. My friend had stacked the deck while we were talking and while seeming to indifferently mix the cards.*

"But what happens if the person you're trying to cheat suddenly decides to switch from Player to Bank?"

"You manage to lose a card," he said.

"How?"

"Lyle," he explained patiently, "when I'm in charge of a game, my crew knows what I want. If I want them to accidentally draw one card too many, they'll understand me and do it."

No major casino will knowingly allow cheating. There is too much investment at stake. Bill Friedman, in his book *Casino Management*, cites Nevada Revised Statute 463.310.4 which gives the gaming commission full power and absolute authority to levy fines of up to $100,000 for the first violation and up to $250,000 for each subsequent violation. The commission also has the right to suspend or revoke a casino license. In one case involving the Aladdin, they exercised their right to stop payments of salaries and profits to the owners.

To sum up, if you owned a casino, would you risk a half-billion-dollar license to win a few dollars or even a few hundred thousand dollars?

You wouldn't.

Still, it isn't possible to control all irregularities. These do occur. One that I recall happened at a major casino several managements back. On weekends and

---

*Protections against this happening to you are: 1) you sit down, but don't play until a new shoe is mixed; and 2) when a new shoe is being prepared, you observe to make sure the Caller laces the cards without skipping any section of the decks.

occasionally on busy weeknights, the swing shift would open two tables. The casino records reflected only one. The money from the second table was divided by the crew, several supervisors, and a cashier. Over a few months' period, the take amounted to several hundred thousand dollars. This, of course, without the knowledge of the owners.

I have no evidence that players were cheated, but in a situation like this, it certainly would benefit those in the collusion to have the table win big.

During its final days, a scandal erupted under the then-management of the Dunes.

This incident took place on the graveyard shift.

A group of players from Hong Kong won a great deal of money in a hurry.

Casino executives suspected cheating and fired four dealers and three supervisors.

The Nevada Gaming Control Board studied videotapes of the game, and at first it was decided that the dealers *had* allowed the gamblers to see the faces of the first four cards and *then* make their bets.

This suspicion was reinforced when more than $16,000 in tips was found in the tip (toke) box.

The gaming board agents obtained search warrants and drilled into four safe deposit boxes in the casino cage. They confiscated $465,440. They also seized another $6,779 in tips that had been withheld from the dealers by the management.

Later the gaming board concluded that it was all a mistake: it wasn't a scam. The money was returned with apologies to all concerned.

There was a question about whether the employees would be rehired, but it soon became academic because the Dunes management changed as often as the government of a Central American banana republic.

Obviously, if *you* have a chance to look at all four cards and then make your bet, you're on the path to financial security. It would be akin to having tomorrow's winning horse-race results or tomorrow's stock-market closings a day in advance!

Veteran casino employees also talk of a time when shaved decks resulted in a cabal of players and dealers cheating the Stardust out of between $300,000 to $400,000.

I have never personally witnessed a case of casino cheating, though I have observed some sly practices by players. A high roller whom we'll call "Mr. X" (because that's what he's called in Ed Thorp's best-selling blackjack book, *Beat the Dealer*) used to place money on the Player section, and if Player won, he would claim it was a wager, but if the Bank won, he'd insist that it was money "to reduce my commissions."

Blatant cheating by a group of players was uncovered recently when two wealthy Hong Kong real-estate executives were arrested on charges that they cheated Las Vegas casinos out of more than $700,000. The pair was part of a seven-person ring that used a false shuffle technique at the minibaccarat tables at the Desert Inn, the MGM Grand, and the Las Vegas Hilton.

Six men and a woman, a group that included three former baccarat dealers, were found guilty of conspiracy, money laundering, and fraud.

What amuses me is that one of the two men, Chi Pang Lee, couldn't have been much of a cheater. He personally dropped $1 million over a two-year period!

John L. Smith, the colorful *Las Vegas Review-Journal* columnist, reported on another Asian group that used a substance to mark the cards. The first time a shoe was dealt, bets were modest. But then when the cards were marked, wagers became large. (Some casinos have a policy of using the eight decks only once and then replacing them. Others use the same cards for several shoes.)

Smith wrote, "With only two standard bets in baccarat, it is not uncommon for an entire table to bet one way or the other."

Suspicion was aroused when the group had an uncanny unbroken series of winning bets.

Casinos have taken steps to avoid having cards marked or daubed. Most casinos now deal blackjack cards face up, not allowing players to touch them.

A personal note: sometimes when I have the shoe and have dealt all four cards, I "sneak a peek" at one of my Bank cards. I sometimes even look at both. Nobody in Vegas has ever objected to this, though there seems to be a taboo against doing just this in Atlantic City casinos.

What's the issue? The cards speak for themselves. The wagers have been placed. The die is cast. The play is automatic. So my peeking at the cards can't change a thing. The fact is, as I've said, the cards could be dealt face up, and nothing would change except that much of the excitement would be missing.

The Beginning
of Wisdom

I'll never understand why otherwise rational human beings go to a casino town to "have fun."

I enjoy life as much as does anyone I know. But I wouldn't visit the barbershop to hear their radio play loud rock music or go to the shoemaker just to glimpse the pretty shoemaker's wife behind the counter.

I go to those respective parlors to have my hair cut and my shoes repaired.

I appreciate the fascination of the struggle. Nine against eight. Seven over six. But is this moment—the struggle against destiny, the intoxication of winning, the drowning feeling that overcomes you when you lose— worth the price you pay? I'm not talking just about the money. The emotional cost, the distortion of values, the twisting of life's meanings—these all have to be totaled before you get your bottom line.

Today's casinos are created by brilliant strategists. They are designed to lull you into escaping reality. Casinos have no clocks, and most have no windows onto the outside world. They are a dark womb. The further they can lead you from reality, the heavier the anesthetic they can inject into your personal value system. After that, it's "a piece of cake" for them to separate you from your dollars.

I once observed that if the casino owners could have their staffs meet you at the entrance, greet you, turn you upside down, and shake out of your pockets whatever cash value you possess, they would have no qualms about then dumping you dead broke into the desert or onto the boardwalk.

I exaggerate not.

As a former casino owner, (I was once a point-holder in the Las Vegas Aladdin) and a longtime friend and confidant of dozens of owners and managers, I assure you that even the most compassionate of them would frantically try to stop a tapped-out player from putting a bullet in his head in the casino lobby. Not because he felt sorry for the loser, but because he knows that blood on the carpet is expensive to remove.

Casino executives don't enjoy my telling you this. Casino executives prefer that you consider them your smiling friends and good buddies. They have careers to pursue and businesses to protect.

Forgive them.

The wolf loves the sheep so much that he eats him.

The casino owners will forgive me for what I've just

written, but they're not as forgiving about my advice to you to hit-and-run. You see, they know that if you hurry in and out, you *could* walk away with some of their cash. But if you're determined to give the casino your money, nothing I can say, no lecture, sermon, or sage advice, will divert you from traveling your self-destructive path.

Let me cite the casino wheel. I've spoken to friends about the bets they lay on that large glass-covered table in front of the Big Six wheel. Although the spinning wheels account for less than 3 percent of the casino's win, they roll up 51 cents worth of hold for every dollar bet on them.

This isn't theory. Let's take the Big Six wheel at Trump Plaza in Atlantic City. In the latest monthly report available (December 1996), the casino's win percentage was 7 percent on baccarat; 11.4 percent at craps; 17 percent at blackjack; and 44.9 percent on the Big Six wheel.

Is this normal? Let's look at the Hilton, Atlantic City. The win percentages were 8.9 percent for baccarat; 19.4 percent for craps; 16.5 percent for blackjack; and 49.5 percent for Big Six.

Does this send some of my less-sophisticated friends scampering for casino games with less odds against them? You bet it doesn't. They smile weakly, shrug, and continue their self-appointed task of giving away their money.

I will not dwell in these pages about the misery and suffering endured by compulsive gamblers. They cheat, they embezzle, they deal in drugs. They'll do *anything* to get a new gambling stake. In his book *Compulsive Gambler*, author Bernie P. tells how he collected donations to pay for his father's funeral and then couldn't resist betting it all on a horse. He lost, of course. Just as William Hoffman, in his *mea culpa, The Loser*, describes how he would build a small fortune at the track and then go into a heavy sweat until he could wager it all on a horse that he knew in his heart of hearts couldn't possibly run faster than a weary walrus.

An analogy to that fellow described a few paragraphs back putting a bullet in his head in the casino lobby is the cigarette addict who keeps putting bullets (cigarettes) in his mouth. They're both addicts. They're both hooked. And they both tell themselves lies that they continue to believe even after their purses are empty (in the case of the gambler) or lung cancer or heart damage has struck (in the case of the smoker).

Anthony Curtis's *Las Vegas Advisor* reports that according to the U.S. Behavioral Risk Factor Surveillance System, nearly 27 percent of all Nevada adults smoke cigarettes. This makes Nevada the fourth smokingest state. Only the citizens of Kentucky, Indiana, and Tennessee are more suicide prone.

I insist that you have to like yourself at least a little to be a winning gambler. Dr. Sirgay Sanger, a Manhattan psychiatrist, treated several compulsive gamblers. He reported that the compulsives had many characteristics in common. They shared low self-esteem, a need to compensate by "feeling big," and a sense of unreality about life.

If you have genuine self-esteem, you don't gamble to

lose. Your pride is involved. You'll play their games to take their money.

The casinos do everything they can to take yours.

Las Vegas, for example, offers you luxurious rooms and suites at moderate prices; spectacular shows, sometimes boasting sixty bare-breasted women (120 tits, count 'em! 120!); the finest chefs preparing fresh high-quality food (most of it flown in daily or shipped in by refrigerator car); tennis and golf courses; and so forth. All these artifacts are part of a carefully thought-out and skillfully executed strategy to persuade you that what you're doing with your money at the tables *isn't insane*. (Most of the time it is.)

The less pleasant you find it, the sooner you'll leave it.

The late Sammy Davis, Jr., once told *Gaming Business* magazine, "In the 1950s and the 1960s . . . you'd be sitting in a restaurant in Beverly Hills, and somebody would say, 'Hey, let's go to Vegas for the weekend.' And everybody would chorus, 'Yeah. Let's go. Let's have some fun.'

"Nobody says that anymore. Because Las Vegas got cold. There's no warmth in that city anymore. It's a cold, computerized no-fun town compared to the city that I once knew, and which I can say, with a minuscule of ego, that I helped to build."

Giving credit where it's due, let me give you an aside on the food. Many years ago, and for an entire decade, I produced a ninety-minute, five-nights-a-week Chinese-language radio program from the top of Manhattan's Chanin Building that was broadcast on WHOM-FM. (No, I'm not Chinese, but, then, neither is blackjack expert and newsletter publisher Stanford Wong.)

My friend Mickey Leffert, who lived in Las Vegas, told me that he loved lichees. Not the dried nuts you get after one dish from column A and two from column B, but the fresh lichee fruit.

I learned from Kang Louis, the lady who was my program's disc jockey, that the first fresh crop of lichees would be arriving from Florida in two days.

When the lichees arrived on Bayard Street, I taxied to New York's Chinatown and bought five pounds of them. I carried them onto the first available plane to Las Vegas.

I checked into a hotel and phoned Mickey at his jewelry emporium only to be told he'd left for the day and wouldn't be at his Rancho Circle home for an hour.

I wandered into the casino. Charles Kandell (one-time hood turned respectable citizen and casino executive) came over to greet me. We chatted for a few minutes, and then I saw a man in the dice pit doing something that made my eyes widen.

Kandell realized that something had captured my sudden attention.

"What's wrong, Lyle?" he asked.

"I'm not sure, Toolie," I replied.

Charlie Kandell's eyes followed my own. A supervisor was standing in the pit, and he was eating fresh lichees!

For one crazy moment, *I was sure that someone had robbed my room!*

And then I realized that my suspicion was pure nonsense. There ain't nothin' that Vegas doesn't get. And as Jerry Stein can tell you (his caviar company sold the finest and most expensive caviar to many of the casinos), *"They get the very best of everything."*

I'd made the 2,238 mile flight for nothing!

Back to the lollipop conditioning. Until you realize that the only reason a casino exists is to take your money, you won't have a real fix on what it's all about.

The only reason for you to enter a casino is to take their money.

Repeat: *the only reason for you to enter a casino is to take their money.*

Ego Massaging

Las Vegas today is an adult Disneyland. Atlantic City is a wasteland by the sea. In both cities, the name of the game is Show Biz.

Attention is paid to casino environment. Careful thought and detail are devoted to lights, temperature, smells, and colors. Atmosphere is everything.

And each day, when midnight rolls around, the "drops" and "holds" are tabulated in the counting room. After which, men and women of no particular talent or distinction are noticeably wealthier. One multimillionaire casino owner who lived on his island conclave couldn't be spoken to after midmorning because he was too drunk. He was also the first casino owner to admit he didn't know the odds against a 6 or an 8 at craps.

I'm reminded of a scene some years ago when a pit

boss thumbed through a fistful of markers and, paraphrasing Sir Winston Churchill, remarked to me, "Never have so many owed so much to so few."

I knew a man who owned a thriving dry-cleaning business. Almost every weekend, he and his wife went to a casino. The casino sent a stretch limousine to carry them from their city to the action. It sent them home in a limousine, too. And in either direction, they watched videocassette movies on the screen of the TV set in the limo.

On some weekends, my dry-cleaning friend lost $10,000 to $20,000.

When I approached his busy shop, I imagined that the sign over the entrance read "Steve Wynn Takes Me to the Cleaners."

He was working for Steve Wynn, but didn't know it. (I don't play at Steve Wynn casinos. They're bad-luck haunts for me.)

The casino exists only to reduce your net worth. Therefore, the *only* reason for you to be in a casino is to take its money.

I can't tell you this too often.

It sounds simple.

It isn't.

That's why the casinos encourage men to bring their wives and girlfriends. That's why they stay in casino cities for long weekends.

If it's a game you want to play, stay home, buy a chessboard or a backgammon set. Or learn bridge.

If it's entertainment you want, read a good book, go to a good movie, watch a good film (or an X-rated one) on your videocassette player. Even better, throw a lavish party. No party can cost you what a serious losing gaming foray could cost.

You'll feel good after the party. And you'll have a lot of people who'll feel good about you, and maybe some of them will invite you to *their* next party.

You *won't* feel good after you piss away several months' income in four hours in a casino. And the only feelings the casino management will have about you is the belief that your checks are good and the hope that you'll go home, work hard, accumulate more money, and bring it with you on your next visit.

Sharing My Experience

Here are some observations I can make after more than thirty-five years of playing baccarat.

1. "Starters" or shills are, on the whole, nice people. They don't affect your chances whatsoever. They're not used as much as they used to be in Vegas, and it's against New Jersey's Casino Control Commission's rules to use them in Atlantic City.

2. Once cards are in the shoe, the die is cast (to quote that often-used cliché from *Bomba the Jungle Boy*). You can't change the flow or sequence of the cards. What happens next depends solely on which side you bet and how much you bet.

3. If you are consistently guessing wrong, sit it
   out for a while. Sit, watch, and don't bet.

4. If you've lost part of your stake and don't feel
   happy at all about the way things are going,
   go. You are under no contract with anyone to
   remain. Go. Take a walk in the fresh air. Go.

That's the single advantage you have over the casinos. They're always there for you to take a shot at their
money, but they can't take a shot at yours, except when
you allow it.

The Hong Kong Connection

They arrive from Hong Kong every week. With the exception of Australia's wealthiest man, Kerry Packer, Asians are the largest gamblers in the history of Las Vegas baccarat.

They are mostly Chinese, and some are quite autocratic.

They're known as the Hong Kong contingent.

In order to give you the most accurate information as opposed to the flotilla of rumors that float around about the Asians, I agreed to alter the names.

The facts are accurate. The names are fictitious.

The leader of the pack is a man who I believe is the biggest gambler in Nevada history. I will call him Mr. Chu. Mr. Chu is a legitimate and highly respected Asian businessman. However, if word of his heavy gambling was to reach Hong Kong, it *could* hurt his image. He uses his personal money—*not* the funds from his billion-dollar organization, as the wretched rumors have implied.

The Hong Kong contingent changes in composition from time to time. Personalities come and go. But always, the leader is Mr. Chu.

There are women in the group who play big. There are men in the group who are known to be even wealthier than Mr. Chu. But no one plays as wildly as he does or for larger stakes.

He is a Las Vegas legend.

Mr. Chu and his companions demand (and receive) the best treatment because, though some in the entourage wager as little as a couple of thousand dollars a hand, others bet $25,000 and $30,000, and Mr. Chu bets Bank or Player for as much as $100,000 a hand.

He has bet $10,000 on Tie and won three Ties in a row. Net profit on such a wager: $240,000.

We aren't talking pennies and quarters. We're talking millions of dollars that go back and forth across the table during any single night of play.

They start playing at about ten P.M. and play for ten to fourteen hours at a stretch. They wear out two or three crews of dealers. Sometimes they will play this way for three consecutive nights, stopping only for dinner and a few hours' sleep. Food is brought to them so they can eat while they play.

When Mr. Chu wins $100,000, he laughs. When he loses $100,000, he laughs.

They often move from casino to casino.

But the sheep give the casinos shudders because they play like foxes, and when they get lucky, they win big.

Most important, they make a special arrangement with the casino. On arriving, they are given full refunds for their first-class round-trip airline fares, from Hong Kong to Las Vegas. This is about $5,370 a person. Thus, the casino hands them as much as $150,000 without blanching.

The casino can win that back on a single baccarat hand.

The group is often given an entire floor in the hotel. In some cases, the ladies are not permitted on the floor. But the rebate deal they have with the casino is interesting. It is based on the combined stake. The casino credits them with 10 percent. Thus, if a combined stake of $20 million is put up, at the end of their visit, the casino will refund $2 million to the group.

The requirement is that the stake must be bet at least twenty times. Thus, with a $20-million stake, bets made during the one, two, or three nights must total at least $400 million.

When they are in action, a casino employee is assigned to stand behind the chair of each player. His job, in part, is to track the amount bet by the player he is monitoring.

In theory at least, the $400-million worth of bets will produce $6 million in casino profits. Deduct the $2-million refund, and the casino would still be ahead four million.

It is exciting to watch this group in action.

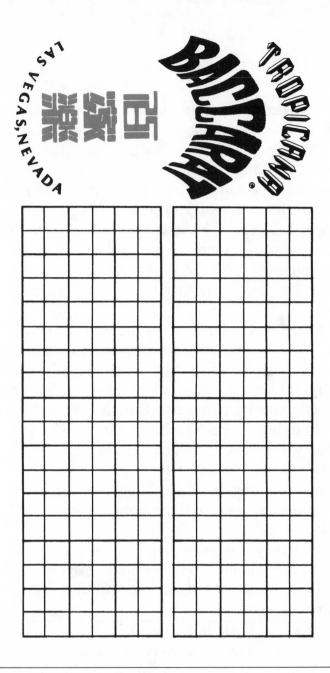

Asians have a different method of keeping score. The casinos supply them with specially designed cards like this one.

For one thing, they rarely use anything smaller than yellow ($1,000) chips. Blacks ($100) are seen only when the so-called commissions are paid and change is given.

Apart from the size of their bets, here are some other ways the Hong Kong contingent is different from you and me:

There is no free choice. If you are part of the group, you don't decide to bet Bank or Player. Rather, you wait for Mr. Chu to decide which side to bet on. You then bet with him.

It would be considered bad manners to bet against him and the group. If, deep in your heart of hearts, you don't feel that's the side to go with, you nevertheless make a token bet. Maybe you use some of those $100 chips that came back as commission change.

Sometimes, if Mr. Chu doesn't feel lucky, he'll ask someone else to select the side.

Their game differs in other ways, too.

Outsiders are not usually permitted to sit at their table. If they inadvertently do, they are quickly intimidated by the size of the wagers.

Also, the shoe doesn't necessarily move when the person holding it doesn't make a pass. Sometimes an entire shoe might be dealt by one person. Sometimes a dealer deals an entire shoe.

Anytime Mr. Chu or one of the others decides that a dealer is "unlucky," that dealer is taken out of the game. If they don't like the shoe, they call for a new shoe. Eight new decks of cards are unwrapped, checked, and shuffled. Management knows better than to utter a peep of protest.

Often it is high drama when the cards are turned over. Mr. Chu will bend them up so slowly that what should take five seconds sometimes takes as long as five minutes to determine the winning side.

He'll chant "baccarat" for the side he is turning over when he wants it to lose. The whole crowd will take up the chant, "Baccarat! Baccarat! Baccarat!"

The dealers sit patiently. They've been well trained. No one receives more considerate treatment than this group.

One of the players was heard to complain that there was too much black in the pit. Black is not a Chinese lucky color. Red is. In swift time, the baccarat pit was painted red and the table covered with a red cloth.

When another player objected to the shills playing with $20 chips ("It cheapens the game," he complained), the green chips were removed immediately, and the lusty-looking ladies were supplied with black ($100) chips.

The group is erratic in its tipping, but sometimes the gentlemen and ladies from Hong Kong will have a large winning streak and will tip the dealers as much as $10,000.

The use of women for pleasure is a taboo as long as the group continues to play. Once the game is over for them, they may do their own thing socially and/or sexually.

On one occasion, a member of the younger set met with one of the buxom blonde shills for an evening of breast exposure and nipple-nipping and afterwards handed her a chip. She thought she was being underpaid until she glanced at it. It was a $20,000 chip.

The shills are not often brought into the game, but some players insist they sit nearby; they may consider one or the other of them lucky.

Luck is everything for this group. Superstition is its middle name. Here are examples to illustrate what I mean.

A young man was standing behind the rope that separates spectators from players. He heard Mr. Chu and his group chanting, "Baccarat! Baccarat! Baccarat!" Having had a few drinks and apparently feeling pretty good, he joined the chorus. This brought smiles to some of the players. They won several hands.

Then they began to lose. Suddenly someone observed that the young man wasn't there. The game was stopped, and a search party went out into the casino to look for him. He was found at a craps table. A $1,000 chip was thrust into his hand, and he was prevailed upon to return to the rope to resume his chanting.

Sometimes, when the players can do nothing right or when a new shoe is being mixed, they'll wander over to the two normal baccarat tables that are functioning. On one occasion, they sat down one at a time until eight of them were in action.

Mr. Chu noticed that a young man at the opposite end of the table was losing most of his bets.

Immediately, he led his group into betting against the young man.

The young man didn't understand any of the Chinese

chatter around him. Nor was he much aware of all the attention people seemed to direct toward his wagers. He was preoccupied. He was losing. He was depressed.

Finally, he lost the last of his chips. He stood up.

"Why you go?" one of the players asked in his limited English.

"Huh? Oh," he said, "I'm going because I'm broke. No money. All gone."

"Sit," Mr. Chu implored.

Sensing that the Chinese man didn't understand, the young man repeated, "No money. All gone." He showed his empty palms.

"Sit!"

It was a command. Puzzled, the young man returned to the empty seat. He was more perplexed when the Chinese contingent contributed chips into a pile, and $5,000 in chips was pushed to him.

"What's this?" he asked.

"You play," said one of the players. "You have money. You play."

The confused man resumed playing. The group resumed betting against him. They continued to win more bets than they lost.

A similar ploy backfired on another occasion.

It happened early one morning after a hard night of holding their own. One of their fellow nationals, whom I'll call Mr. Eng, was known to all of them, but he wasn't one of Mr. Chu's group. He wandered in, greeted everybody, and seated himself at their table.

Mr. Eng wagered on Player. Mr. Chu bet on Bank, and of course, his friends all supported his luck by betting with him on Bank.

Player won.

Mr. Eng then bet on Bank. Mr. Chu bet on Player, and immediately and faithfully, all the others bet Player.

Bank won.

This went on for several hands.

Finally, it was agreed that Mr. Eng was running very lucky. They weren't. So after much eye language and some whispering, they decided to "steal his luck."

Chu bet on Player. Eng bet Bank.

Just before the first card was dealt, the entire group pushed their bets into Bank.

Eng was too fast for them! He drew his chips back to Player.

Player won.

It was all very frustrating!

On a couple of back-to-back visits, the 10 percent refund coupled with some lucky streaks made the group a big winner.

The casino owners were more than annoyed. Petty bickering began. The casino claimed the 10 percent was too much. Management insisted that the players bet on every hand.

There was a lot of arguing. Many in the group felt this was a deliberate strategy by the casino management to upset Mr. Chu because he rarely won bets when he was angry.

But the group was much needed.

One of the shift bosses told me, "If they keep coming here every month, I'm going to consider believing in a god. Maybe several of them!"

When it was known that the Hong Kong contingent was patronizing a rival casino, Caesars Palace didn't sit on its hands. It produced a lavish Chinese show to lure the Chinese players from the other hotel.

Never had a show been so widely advertised! Every taxi in town and every bus carried billboards heralding the fact that for five nights only, the Chinese opera, direct from Hong Kong, would perform at Caesars Palace.

The showroom *wouldn't* be packed. Wayne Newton's fans were not going to stampede over to Caesars Palace to see this one. But, obviously, all that the Palace owners wanted was to attract just a few of the Asian baccarat big bettors.

Caesars Palace made one error. The placards and posters on the cabs, buses, and billboards all over town were only in English.

Most of the Hong Kong visitors spoke and read only Chinese.

♠ ♦ ♥ ♣

During one period, the Hong Kong contingent varied from their routine by making four visits to Atlantic City. They didn't like it. The hotels lacked elegance. The food and room service weren't up to Las Vegas standards.

In addition, on their initial visit, they had to use racks full of chips because the highest denomination in action were the gray $5,000 chips.

Las Vegas needs those bilious businessmen from Hong Kong. It dreads the day when they get tapped out or find a more appealing form of gaming.

Casinos sometimes have more elaborate offices in Asia than they do in New York or Los Angeles. You do your deep-sea fishing where the fish swim.

The Arabs (who always favored London, anyway) have vanished. The Mexicans were hoisted by their petard of plummeting peso value, although there's still one player who is flown by private hotel plane to the Taj Mahal and is allowed to wager as much as $110,000 a hand. He has been known to lose as much as $4 million on a weekend.

Doctors and bankers? They've taken their gambling to the stock market.

Incidentally, Las Vegas never had the size of Arab action that the Middle Easterners gave to London. One of the notorious big players, Adnan Khashoggi, was so slow to redeem his markers that the casino decided that, despite its desperate need for big players, Adnan's action, coupled with the snail's-pace redemption of his markers, wasn't worth what it cost to host him and his entourage.

Ladbroke's in London had a $200,000 chip that was often in action on a single number when the Arabs played roulette there.

But those days are rapidly fading memories.

Back to Baccarat

Of all the games in the casino, baccarat vies with craps as my favorite. (And, as I have often remarked, blackjack is my least favorite.)

Baccarat has advantages over casino craps. For one thing, decisions are quicker. No waiting for that 3.5 average rolls of two cubes before you know whether you've won or lost your line bet.

For another thing, the range of the wager you can make is wonderfully wide. In no other game can you put down $20 or $100,000 on the Bank or Player side and win or lose it in less time than it took you to read this sentence.

Nor do you need to be the heavy bettor at the table to have your share of thrills. It's a strange feeling for you to be the only person at a table to bet one side, maybe for only $20. Your side wins, and $40,000 of other people's wagers are swept from the table even as you're paid your $20 win.

Bet Player and win and you've doubled your stake. Bet Bank and win and you've added 95 percent to it.

In no other game can you make ten losing bets in a row and then make one daring big one and recover your losses—and maybe show a profit as well.

It's clean and it's swift.

It's swift and it's clean.

Baccarat has no purpose different from that of the other casino money-traps. Don't let the formal attire of the dealers or the elegant atmosphere persuade you otherwise.

It's the casino's "class game" and the one that can be played for the most money per decision. But it's also just another game designed to extract profits for the casino's coffers.

♠ ♦ ♥ ♣

Baccarat is becoming more popular every day.

In the 1960s when there were only a few tables in all of Las Vegas, I used to watch the Dostoevsky-like shills who sat for hours turning over cards and waiting for the first "real player" to take a seat.

Two decades later, I watched five tables working simultaneously in Caesars Palace—and half a dozen customers queued up, waiting for empty seats so they could play.

I remind you again that one thing in your favor is that the casino is always there for you to take a shot at their money, but they can't take a shot at yours except when *you* decide to allow it. That's an important advantage: you can start and stop when *you* want to. They must play all the time.

Remember: if three Player or Bank wins come up in a row, your proper move is either to bet on a fourth in the sequence or not to bet at all.

Just as a monkey could throw the dice, as I mentioned earlier, a poodle or a pig could be trained to deal a baccarat shoe. Nevertheless, we humans often get strong feelings about other people at the table. If we don't care for someone's looks or style, we tend to bet against that person. If we like 'em, we sometimes bet with 'em, even against our own strong instincts!

When the shoe travels to you and Player has won the last three hands, you *must* bet Player. You'll win as often as you lose. The fact that you're holding the shoe doesn't change the face of a single card in it. (God has not taken time out from counting the proceeds in that Big-Collection-Plate-in-the-Sky to look down and turn that queen of spades into a nine of clubs just because you once won brownie points in a Boy Scout troop.

(Don't believe in "the power of prayer." Even if every human on earth got down on his or her knees and prayed for a nine of clubs as the next card, the queen of spades would still come up the queen of spades.)

So, even though it "goes against your grain"—bet Player. It can be a small bet. If you lose, you'll still have the shoe, and now you can bet Bank.

If it is psychologically impossible for you to bet against yourself while you're dealing, simply pass the shoe when it comes to you. It will come around again.

There is more drama at a baccarat table than almost any other place you can name.

I used to watch an Asian whom dealers called "Mr. T." He was Indonesian. I found him at the tables on at least one out of every two visits I made to Las Vegas.

He dropped *millions* of dollars. Literally.

He was so colorful that the *Las Vegas Sun* published an article about him.

I recall $5,000 chips flowing through his hands like spring water.

"That makes a million, Mr. T.," the dealer said one evening.

The next morning, I happened to be at the table struggling to recover my paltry four- or five-thousand-dollar loss, when he sat down again.

"Give me two hundred," he said.

"Did he win his million back?" I surreptitiously inquired of the dealer who sat at my right.

"No," he whispered, shaking his head. "This is the start of *another* million!"

Mr. T. lost the second million before I left the table. It was then that I heard it said that he owned one of Macao's largest gambling casinos. While he lingered in America, it was being run by his sons.

I couldn't reconcile this. Someone who understood odds, percentages, and the inexorable victory of the house nevertheless playing into the face of it. Why?

I asked Caesars Palace baccarat supervisor Gene Ficke, "Gene, why does he do it? How do you figure it? I'm baffled."

"It used to puzzle me, too," Gene said. "What I've come to believe is that since he has apparently conquered everything he ever challenged, he's just not going to let this game beat him."

Mr. T. wore a toupee that usually sat lopsided on his head. It appeared to be something that could have cost him no more than eight dollars American money or that maybe he picked up in a used-rug sale.

On the other hand, I understand that there is an old Indonesian saying that "Money makes an ugly girl pretty."

No doubt about that. For many years, Mr. T. was the prettiest player at the Caesars Palace baccarat table.

I Sue for Libel

I want to tell you more about my Rule of Three, but first let me tell you a story.

When my first gaming book was published, it received a glowing review in *Rouge et Noir*. This sophisticated gaming newsletter gave it one of its rare "Highly recommended" ratings.

Hank Greenspun wrote in his *Las Vegas Sun*, "I've read many gambling books over the years . . . but I don't think I can classify any of them as really good books until this one. . . . It's worth its weight in gold to those determined to win."

My old New School for Social Research classmate Mario Puzo read the manuscript and found himself so inspired that he flew to Las Vegas and won $10,000 which he came home with. He gave me permission to include in our ads his statement: "The only book which ever gave me a winning day in Vegas!"

Not bad, eh?

Malcolm Forbes wrote that I was "The book world's most colorful publisher" and was impressed enough to describe my book in the pages of *Forbes* as "Great reading."

The whipped cream on the cake came from Harry Reid. Reid was then a commissioner of gaming in the state of Nevada. He's now a United States senator. He volunteered an unsolicited testimonial in which he said, ". . . if one must gamble, then the reading of this book is a must."

Meanwhile, I kept waiting for a review in what was then the leading gaming magazine, *Gambling Times*.

Silence.

Bob Salomon, the publishing company's executive vice president, queried the magazine's editor.

He was given five minutes of double-talk on why the magazine couldn't review the book.

It reminded me of a similar situation many years ago when Nicolas Darvas wrote his national best-seller *How I Made Two Million Dollars in the Stock Market*. Nick recommended the weekly financial newspaper *Barron's* as "must" reading. As a result, *Barron's* circulation doubled and then tripled.

One would expect *Barron's* to be eternally grateful to Darvas for making their weekly a smashing success.

One would be wrong.

Barron's refused all advertising for the second Darvas book, *Wall Street—The Other Las Vegas*.

Why?

Because that book likened the stock exchange to a giant casino and pointed out that whether stock prices went up or stock prices went down, the casino (stock broker) got its percentage (commission).

Since the pages of *Barron's* were larded with advertising by brokerage houses, *Barron's* had decided not to risk offending its golden geese.

A similar situation was happening with *Gambling Times*. After all, my book said flatly that there are no mathematical systems that can defeat the built-in negative expectation in every casino wager. *Gambling Times* was a magazine peppered with advertising for books and services that promised "systems" to beat casino games.

A *Gambling Times* spokesman finally told Bob Salomon that the magazine didn't intend to review the book because its publisher "didn't like the book and didn't want to give it a bad review."

Strange. Since when does a magazine not publish "bad" reviews as well as "good" ones? (Can you imagine The *New York Times* not reviewing a Broadway show because its theater critic didn't like it?)

We persevered. And apparently some of my fans among their readers wrote to them, too.

I was now receiving a flow of mail from delighted readers of my book containing statements like, "I'm a lifetime gambler, and yours is the most interesting and authentic book ever to come along," and "Your book has changed my perception of casinos. I wish I had it four years ago—I'd have avoided lots of mistakes and saved lots of money!"

One day I opened my mail and began to read what

looked to be my first complaint.

This letter was three pages long, neatly handwritten. It started out by saying that the writer bought the book for $20 and after reading it, decided it was a ripoff. It went on to describe a recent visit to Atlantic City, where he had happened to bring along his copy of my book. His gambling started off badly. Suddenly, he recalled my advice to walk away from losing streaks. He retired to his hotel room and reread the book. His letter ended with the surprise statement that its writer had left Atlantic City a $1,500 winner and "I want you to know that your book is the best investment I've ever made!"

Still we waited.

At last *Gambling Times* came out of the closet. It didn't review the book. Instead, it published a full-page editorial attacking it.

The editorial didn't merely say the book was a bad book. It said it was "a fraud."

I launched my publishing empire with money that I won in libel actions against Broadway gossip columnist Walter Winchell, the Hearst publishing empire, and the now-defunct scandal magazine *Confidential*, so I consider myself something of a libel expert. But the laws have since been interpreted on the side of more freedom for the press (something I favor), and I wanted an expert opinion.

My good friend and attorney, Albert B. Gerber*,

---

*Gerber wrote the best-selling Howard Hughes biography, *Bashful Billionaire*, as well as several other books including the more recent *The Book of Sex Lists*.

asked the noted libel expert Elmer Gertz for a professional opinion. Gertz practices what he teaches. He collected $476,808.09 from Robert Welch and the John Birch Society for their erroneously calling him "a communist."

Gertz supported my belief that the magazine's editorial went beyond fair comment and was actionable.

I sued *Gambling Times* and its publisher, Stanley Sludikoff, for libel.

♠ ♦ ♥ ♣

Now imagine a change of scene.

I was a finalist in a baccarat tournament at an Atlantic City hotel.

There were four players in the finals. I should have been the tournament champion, but I made a dumb move which I'll describe later.

The bottom line was that I blew it and only came in second. (Since then I have won tournaments with prizes ranging from $75,000 to $125,000.)

I'd never met Stanley Sludikoff. So, when a stranger came up to commiserate with me on my dumb move, I was cordial. Then he told me he was Sludikoff. Our conversation promptly turned to his editorial against my book. He insisted that his comments had been fair and accurate.

I disagreed.

We strolled through the casino. A woman approached me. "Mr. Stuart, I don't know how to thank you! Last month my husband won $16,000, *and he came home with it*! And it was all because of your book!"

Sludikoff winced.

Minutes later, a young fellow stopped me. "You can't imagine how your book has changed my approach to gambling," he said. "Especially your Rule of Three."

In less than ten minutes, we were approached again. "Mr. Stuart, you don't know me," the elderly man said, "but I want to shake your hand. I own a restaurant near Lincoln Center in New York City. Until I read your book, I was practically working for the casinos. Now I sometimes win. More important, I never suffer those big losses I used to have, thanks to your Rule of Three. Here's my card. I'd love you and your family to come in for a meal as my guest."

By now, Sludikoff had paled.

I chuckled and turned to him. "If you didn't know better, you'd believe I hired a bunch of actors to say all these nice things about my book!"

Stanley didn't appreciate the humor. He looked grim.

"Can we settle your lawsuit?" he asked.

We retired to the coffee shop. We agreed that I would receive $12,500 worth of free advertising in *Gambling Times* and I would drop the lawsuit.

Within days, our lawyers exchanged releases, and the matter was disposed of.

However Sludikoff's attorney neglected to withdraw his motion on the case. Two weeks later (in what I consider a wrong decision), Judge H. Lee Sarokin of the United States District Court ruled on my suit.

Judge Sarokin said in part, "If the plaintiffs have the right to purvey pleasant dreams, the defendants have an equal right to proclaim that they are nightmares."

Judge Sarokin dismissed the suit.

In a subsequent issue of his *Gambling Times*, Stanley Sludikoff, writing under his pen name of Stanley Roberts, published a "new opinion" of my book.

"I can tell you," he wrote, "that Lyle Stuart plays exactly the way he describes in his book. Therefore, it is a fair assumption that his book accurately reflects his own experiences at the gaming tables. . . .

"I found Lyle to be a warm and generous human being. When he met a young man who had obviously lost a sum of money which he apparently could not afford, I saw Lyle give this fellow enough money to help him out of a serious dilemma. To the best of my knowledge, that person had been a perfect stranger who recognized Lyle from the photograph on his book jacket. . . .

"What do I think of Lyle Stuart? He'd be welcome as a guest in my home anytime he comes to Los Angeles."

Stanley kept to his agreement and published $12,500 worth of our ads in *Gambling Times*. They pulled well.

All those appreciative readers who approached me in the casino that day helped enrich me by $12,500.

Keep in mind that two of those who expressed their gratitude for my book talked about my Rule of Three.

Junket and
Other Puddings

Casino junket organizer "Big Julie" Weintraub once said, "The guy who invented gambling was brilliant, but the guy who invented chips was a genius."

To which I'll add, "The person who invented the rules for baccarat was an even-greater genius than the man who invented chips and even smarter than the man who conceived the junket!"

Baccarat is a simple game. It's a heads-or-tails toss of a coin. Yet the mathematics are diabolically clever.

If you sit at the table* long enough, there is no way

*Speaking of leaving the table, Roger King is cofounder of King World which syndicates such TV hit shows as *Oprah* and *Jeopardy!*. He visited the Sands in Atlantic City in March of 1997 and arranged for a high-stakes blackjack game. He won $1.2 milto avoid the house grinding you down with its subtle percentage.

Please read the above paragraph again.

Now read it for the third time!

It is the most important insight into casino baccarat that I can offer you. I shudder to recall the number of times when, violating my own rules, I failed to leave the table when I was ahead and as a result, lost most or all of the money back. It's pure and simple: *the secret to successful gambling is knowing when to quit.*

Gaming is not unlike the stock market where for a century they've said, "A bull can make money, and a bear can make money, but a pig can never make money."

Greed can be your undoing. It has been mine all too often.

When you're ahead, take your winnings and run. Don't try to win the whole casino in one sitting. (You wouldn't know what to do with it anyway. Who wants to assume a payroll and overhead of a couple of hundred thousand dollars a day?)

Twenty years ago when I wrote and published *Casino Gambling for the Winner*, I planned to title it *Hit and Run*. Hitting-and-running is the *only* consistent winning approach to gaming that I know.

It's the way I won $166,505 (after all expenses) on ten consecutive visits to Las Vegas—every one a win-

---

lion. Then he insisted that the casino raise the limits on his maximum bet. They wouldn't, so he walked out with his winnings. He knew when to leave the table!

ning visit. It's the way I walked away from one Atlantic City baccarat pit with $130,000 that I won on one shoe. Had I not successfully defeated my own urge to play "just one more shoe," it's likely that amount would have been greatly reduced.

Why then do I consider baccarat a game that gives you a better shot than the widely publicized blackjack? Look at casino winning reports, and you'll see that blackjack is a steady and reliable winner for casinos. I don't know a single instance where any casino in New Jersey or Nevada reported a quarterly loss at their blackjack tables, but there have been several instances where casinos had to tell stockholders that earnings were disappointing or nil because of negative results in their baccarat pit.

For example, the Frontier lost money at baccarat every month for five months. Other more recent losers have included the MGM Grand, the Mirage, the Desert Inn, and Caesars Palace.

In the 1960s when Milton Prell opened the Aladdin Hotel and Casino on the Las Vegas Strip, he invited me to invest. Those were the days when it was widely believed that most casinos kept three sets of books: one for the IRS, one for the partners, and the real one.

Prell was reputed to be an exception. The story was that he needed only two sets: the reports that were shown to the partners and the set for the IRS.

I bought one point (1 percent of the stock).

While my application was pending, I was one of three players who won more than a quarter-of-a-million dollars at the Aladdin baccarat table in two days. The

Aladdin promptly closed its baccarat pit and didn't open it again for nine weeks.

"We don't understand the game," casino manager Gil Gilbert confessed to me. "It's too dangerous for us."

Yet they didn't consider it dangerous when one man hit them for $10,000 four separate times within twenty-four hours at their Keno game. This was the day after the casino opened for business.

"It's an aberration," Gilbert said about the Keno winner. "We know that we'll recover all that money in time."

In those days, baccarat table limits were $2,000.

Caesars Palace pioneered the way to a $4,000 maximum bet for everyone (and $8,000 for Frank Sinatra and friends). Then to $8,000 for everyone. Today they retain a leadership position with a high limit for any player (negotiable with the management), while downtown, the ordinary maximum wager in baccarat at Binion's Horseshoe is $50,000. Again, negotiable. Your limit can be as much as $1 million if that's the amount of your first bet.

Limits change with the sunsets. Years ago the Dunes (since leveled to the ground) offered high rollers a $60,000 limit per hand. Caesars countered with an $80,000 limit, if arrangements were made. The Dunes responded by announcing that "If you play for cash instead of credit, the Dunes will let you set your own limit."

Casinos know that publicized winners are wonderful sucker-bait. They help to hook thousands of players who are wishful dreamers. If a housewife can insert $8 in a slot machine and win $2 million—why can't it happen to you? Never mind that the odds may be thirty or forty million to one. *She* won, didn't she?

Thus, Caesars Boardwalk Regency in Atlantic City was delighted to take full-page ads in magazines such as *Playboy* with the headline, *"The $2,200,000 baccarat conquest."*

The full-color illustrated page was a baccarat shoe on a green-felt baccarat table from which a king of spades and a nine of diamonds had been dealt the Bank. And it contained the following message:

> He was the solitary player at baccarat table two, betting $100,000 per hand. 45 minutes after sitting down he got up with $1,823,500. That was on Saturday at 1:45 A.M. Sunday morning he returned to the scene of his success and won another $387,900. In all, he returned home with over $2.2 million.
>
> It could only happen at Caesars.

The last claim isn't quite valid. I have seen a visitor from Hong Kong win $3,300,000 in three hours at the Desert Inn. And I've watched another visitor lose at least three million in two days.

The Hong Kong $3,300,000 winner quit after announcing, "I'm hungry."

The management offered to bring food right to the table. Caviar. Shark fin's soup. Baked human being, I suppose, if that was his preference. Anything he wanted.

No, he explained. He had an urge for a Wendy's hamburger, and he wanted to eat it hot off the griddle.

We all know that there is no free lunch. Life doesn't dish out bowls full of something for nothing. We know it, and yet those thousands of high rollers who've been seduced into flying to Las Vegas on "free" junkets still believe, in an act of wishful thinking, that casinos give them something for free.

The underrated film, *Casino*, includes a scene about a visitor from Asia who plays for millions, but gets his kicks out of packing hotel towels and soap in his suitcase.

Comedian Bill Cosby describes the kind of player I'm talking about. Says Cosby, "He gets excited about the fact that he doesn't have to pay for anything. That thrills him. The man could own real estate worth $100 million and bring with him a credit line of $250,000, which he is willing to gamble and lose and sign his name to the check, but he'll be damned if he's going to pay $130 for dinner for two at a casino restaurant."

To each his own.

I paid for a casino hotel room only once in my life. That was at Resorts International in Atlantic City when it first opened and offered "the only game in town." The casino was so mobbed with people fighting for places at slot machines and at the table games that I couldn't wait to get out.

I've paid only once for plane tickets to Vegas without recovering their cost at the cashier's cage. Why? Because I play for high enough stakes to be considered a traditional lollipop. The exception happened at the Mirage. I was Steve Wynn's guest, even though we were involved in suing each other over my publication the John L. Smith book, *Running Scared.*

I was scheduled to meet with Wynn and his attorneys in his executive offices. Wynn was unhappy because Smith's book revealed and documented the fact that at various times in his career, Wynn had associated with shady people who were mob connected. This contradicted the clean preppy image he'd spent millions to project.

Because of the scheduled meeting with Wynn, I had limited time for gambling. I played some blackjack at $3,000 a hand for a half-hour or so. When I requested my airfare, I was told my play hadn't been long enough to justify it.

I've never stayed at or played at a Wynn casino since. Steve Wynn is prospering, and so am I. We both get along fine without each other!

Back to the subject of junkets. Just a few days ago, the MGM Grand invited me to fly to Vegas on their private plane with its catered menu.

Not for me.

I have a strong instinct against being herded. I don't want anyone to tell me when I must arrive and when I must depart. And so, I never fly on junkets.

To walk away with casino money, you must feel free to walk *anytime*. And you also have to feel free *not* to gamble if that's the way your instinct moves you.

Too often have I seen men and women on junkets who felt obligated to play for hours in their host casino to insure that they'd be comped then and in the future.

If the price of your liberty to come and go, to play or not to play, and to hit-and-run means giving up the free airfare and the comped room, food, and beverage, by all means give them up.

You'll feel better about doing what you want to do when you want to do it rather than what they want you to do.

They want you to give them as much of your money as they can take from you in the shortest possible time.

What's your response?

The decision, dear reader, is yours.

A Miracle Morning

I was staying at the Las Vegas Tropicana. I'd lost $12,000 and was tired. At about 11:30 P.M., I had the good sense to return to my room for a room-service supper and some sleep.

I awoke at 4 A.M.

I hadn't had much sleep, but I felt refreshed and recharged.

I was booked on a morning flight to Los Angeles.

First, I mapped out my strategy. I would play cautiously. I would play exactly two shoes. Then, whatever happened, I'd manage another two hours of rest, and if the urge was there, I'd still have time to play two more shoes.

When I went downstairs, a shoe had almost ended. I called for $10,000 worth of chips and sat at the table, but didn't bet. Soon it was time for the dealers to mix a new shoe.

The man directly to my right looked familiar. "Weren't you playing here last night?" I asked.

"I haven't left the table," he said mournfully. "You wouldn't believe the cards. They've been awful! It's been nothing but chop-chop. There hasn't been one good run."

"I'm amazed that you lasted this long," I said.

Later the fellow told me he'd moved to Vegas about five months before and was in the business of selling diamonds for investment.

I played the first shoe very cautiously. Too cautiously. When it was dealt out, I'd won about $1,700. Not bad for forty-five minutes work and a choppy shoe. But I recognized that I needed to increase the size of my wagers if I was going to make any real dent in the more than $10,000 I was still behind.

I did.

This second shoe wasn't much improvement over the first. But I won more hands than I lost, and I managed to get ahead another $5,500 before the shoe passed to me.

I bet $4,000 on Bank, and I dealt myself a winner. Then the white plastic card came out, and the Caller announced, "The next hand will be the last hand of this shoe."

I was forced to make a decision.

What if I won the last hand and was therefore entitled to start the new shoe when it was ready? What of my promise to myself to quit after two shoes?

I bet $3,000 on the last hand.

I won.

I was now ahead almost $4,000 for the visit. But I had to deal with a dilemma.

In those days, I drank a lot of Diet Coke with lemon at the table. So, at the end of a shoe, I felt compelled to hurry to the latrine. I deliberately avoided the nearest men's room and selected one at the farthest end of the casino.

I made a decision and then evaluated it. I kept hearing my neighbor's complaint about there not having been any streaks. I decided to violate my strategy of leaving now that I'd played two full shoes. However, in my mind, I set up a built-in stop-loss mechanism.

After the shuffle, I would take the new shoe. I would make a large bet. If I won, I would keep betting. But as soon as I lost one hand, I would leave immediately.

I took the new shoe.

My scorecard is reproduced on the next page.

I bet $5,000 on Bank on the first hand and won it.

Remember that I was playing defensively.

My second bet was $2,700. After I paid the $250 "vig" on the first hand and even if I lost this wager, I'd be more than $2,000 ahead for the new shoe.

I was already happy that I'd stayed. There was no way that I would not be a winner for taking the shoe.

I dealt a Tie.

I bet Tie after a Tie. It's a foolish bet, but for no rational reason, I've made money with it.

So I bet $200 on the Tie and cut my Bank bet to $2,500.

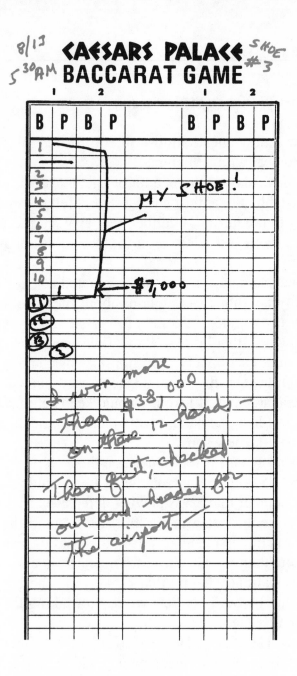

This one will always recapture happy memories!

Bank side won the next hand.

I was still cautious. I pulled back the $2,500 winnings and kept my wager at $2,500.

I won again.

The fellow to my right became excited. "Maybe you're on a streak!" he said hopefully.

"Maybe," I said.

He increased the size of his bet.

I added $500 to my own.

I won again. I added another $1,000 to the wager.

I won again.

My analysis of several hundred complete shoes indicates that on streaks, the fifth hand is the most difficult to get passed. I kept my wager at $4,000 and bet a couple of black chips ($200) for the dealers.

The guy to my right now had a high stack of green ($25) chips riding on me.

I won the sixth hand.

I bet $5,000.

I won.

The next three hands seemed to take only seconds. I was eager to deal. $6,000. I won. $7,000. I won. $7,000. I won.

Meanwhile, the fellow to my right was too slow on two occasions. Twice his hand was full of chips and hesitantly moving to the Bank box when the Caller announced, "Cards are out. No more bets."

I'd made ten Bank hands in a row.

Now I bet $7,000 again.

I lost the eleventh decision. The hand was one of those cliff-hangers. The first four cards were pictures. I dealt a deuce to Player and an ace to myself.

Player over Bank 2 to 1.

The shoe passed to the fellow at my right.

Emotionally, I wanted to bet with him. Every fiber of my instinct assured me the Player hand was a temporary interruption of the streak.

I controlled myself by recalling the pledge I'd made to myself.

He made three Bank hands while I watched. It bothered me less than I thought it would.

We left the table to breakfast together. My ten-Bank streak had turned him from big loser to small winner. But those bets that he didn't get onto the cloth on time and the scared bets he made when he himself dealt the shoe cost him what would have been a lovely profit for his long hours at the baccarat table.

He kept mourning his hesitation.

I repeated what my good friend Mickey Leffert told me two decades before. It was that he didn't believe anyone could live in Las Vegas and survive long if he gambled, drank excessively, or was a woman chaser.

I mentioned this in passing, but the man assured me that he was a careful player and usually won a little money and left the tables.

Me? I was one happy fellow.

I'd made a $50,000 turnaround.

I'd won more than $38,000!

Even that didn't please me as much as the fact that *I had kept the promise I had made to myself*. I had quit after one losing hand.

If you can set your strategy and *stick to it*, you'll improve greatly your chances of becoming a winner.

The Man from Playboy

Some years ago, Victor Lownes flew to New York from London. I met him at Kennedy Airport, and we drove for nearly three hours to a house my wife bought as a weekend escape for us. It's located in Stuyvesant, New York, and overlooks the Hudson River.

There, cut off from phone calls, mail, and visitors, we worked together without interruption to revise a book by Victor that had previously been published in England.

The British publisher titled it *Playboy Extraordinary*. We called it *The Day the Bunny Died*.

In its pages, Victor talked about the near-collapse of the Playboy empire when it lost its license to operate casinos in London.

The story is a fascinating tale of the bumbling executives and fumbling flunkies surrounding Hugh Hefner.

During the time we were together, Victor and I had a chance to discuss casino gaming in depth.

The London casino he opened and directed was, in its time, the most profitable casino in the world. It threw off a profit of something in excess of $30 million dollars a year. (For a time, Victor was listed in the *Guinness Book of Records* as Britain's highest-paid business executive.)

Victor doesn't gamble. Even when he plays backgammon (he beats me regularly), he won't play with anyone his equal, for that would pose the threat of a loss. He even stopped playing with Hugh Hefner when the latter's game improved.

Lownes was unceremoniously fired when Hugh Hefner had someone telephone him from California at 4 A.M. London time to tell him he was terminated. Playboy would sacrifice Victor to save the Playboy casino license. (They lost both Victor and the license.)

At the time of his dismissal, Victor had managed to stash aside coffee-and-cake money. He'd accumulated a tidy nest egg which last year threw off a million-and-a-half dollars from the stock market.

What does Victor Lownes think of gambling?

"Expensive entertainment," he says with finality.

Diversion. Amusement. Costly thrills.

But does the player ever win?

"There's no way to beat the house out of its inexorable percentages," he will tell you.

"How about the people who actually walk out of the casino winners?"

"Our best customers!" he declared. "Those can be considered as having taken out short-term, high-interest casino loans. We know the winners will return because they believe they've discovered the secret of defeating the casino. They're hooked! In the long run, only the casino wins."

It's a depressing thought.

Do the winners return?

Of course.

Do they lose back what they've won?

Often the answer is "yes and then some."

"Make sure the customers are happy" is the casino philosophy.

Never mind that they are winners. That's a temporary aberration.

"Make them happy," say the strategists.

There was the time a player had lost a lot of money at baccarat. He asked for a new shoe even though the current shoe was half-dealt.

The pit boss okayed the request.

The player had enough money for one large wager. He won. He left the table thirty minutes later some $380,000 ahead.

Management was undisturbed. "Let him enjoy it," the pit boss said, really meaning it. "He'll be back."

A young Japanese player named Mizumo arrived one day with a $200,000 bankroll. He lost $190,000 of it at baccarat. Then his fortune changed. He bet his last $10,000 and won. He had a winning streak in which he played aggressively and won back the $190,000 and $600,000 more.

The management at some casinos would have gone into a deep funk. Perhaps if the owner was a Kirk Kerkorian type, he would have barred the player from returning or at least muttered incantations against all the dealers involved.

But this pit boss was a veteran who understood gaming. "He's got the monkey on his back. Every winner has. He'll return, and he'll give us back the money. Just be sure that, for now, he is treated well and gets everything he wants."

Pearl Harbor for Mr. Mizumo came sooner than anyone had anticipated. Three weeks later, he phoned from Hawaii to announce that he was returning.

"Get my suite ready for me!" he said cheerfully. "I'm coming back, and this time I'm going to win the whole damned casino!"

"How much are you bringing?" his host couldn't help asking.

"Just enough! The same lucky two hundred grand I came with last time," Mizumo said.

A special suite was prepared. A Japanese cook was employed to prepare Japanese food for him.

Mizumo arrived with a broad smile on his face. For several sessions, he won and lost modest amounts. Then the slippage began. He lost the $200,000. He wired Tokyo for more money.

He lost back $582,000 of the $600,000 he'd won.

It was the same old story, but it was new to him.

I've won a lot of money. Over the past forty years, have I won more than I lost? Not at all. I've lost more than I've won. I don't lie about my gambling. The first step to self-deception is lying to others about your gains and losses.

When I made a national tour of television, radio, and the press for Random House, I insisted on starting every interview with, "Don't gamble. People who gamble are crazy. But if you *must* gamble, learn everything you possibly can about the game you intend to play."

I titled my previous gaming book *Winning at Casino Gambling* because compulsive gamblers are like compulsive cigarette smokers. They're losers who don't want to win.

I hope and trust that you do. And that you're aware of all the odds against you, whether you gamble, or smoke, or do both.

Paying Markers

Atlantic City's gaming establishments, casino-for-casino, now do as much business as the best of their Nevada cousins. They have an edge: they collect most of the money they win.

In days gone by, Nevada casino owners complained about the difficulties of their task. First, they had to attract the player. Then they had to win his money. Then they had to collect what they'd won.

In Atlantic City, credit restrictions have been relaxed slightly, but they are still tight. You give them your personal check. Third-party checks are not acceptable, even if they are made payable to you from the United States government.

For years, Nevada casino executives have tried to work out a more effective way to collect gambling losses. There have been scenarios such as what happened at one

Strip hotel when the players knew the hotel was about to either change hands or go under. They signed lots of markers, never intending to pay them. If they lost, tough. If they won, they collected the cash. It was fun while it lasted.

At long last, Nevada legislators decided to deal with the problem of overdue markers and of those players who ignored their obligations altogether.

Contrary to myth, casinos don't send tough guys to break the arms and legs of people who don't pay. They do employ collectors, and some of these chaps are most imaginative.

Let's say your name is Frank Jones. You owe $2,000, and you've decided not to honor your obligation because you know that Nevada gambling debts aren't legally collectible outside of Nevada.

The collector's campaign begins.

No one bothers you. But at 2 A.M., a telephone call awakens your neighbor. "Frank? Frank Jones? I'm calling about the $2,000 you owe the Golden Rainbow casino."

"I'm not Frank Jones!" the neighbor explodes. "He lives in the house next door."

"Oh, I'm so sorry," the collector says.

The next morning, your neighbor tells you that someone woke him up about a $2,000 gambling debt.

That night, the neighbor on the other side of you is awakened at 4 A.M. with the same request.

Two days later, your boss is called. You're sitting in the next office, but the collector asks, "Do you know where we can locate Frank Jones? He owes the Golden Rainbow casino $2,000."

Trouble in River City. Not only have you been humil-iated with your neighbors, but now your employer has been alerted to the fact that you are a gambler. Perhaps you're living above your income? Maybe it's time to check your petty-cash vouchers? Your boss begins to perceive you in a new light.

Or, imagine that they hold your marker for $2,000. You feel safe. You have only $1,640 in the bank. If they try to put the $2,000 marker through, it will go bouncy-bouncy.

Or so you thought.

The goal of the collector is to collect. His expertise helps him discover that you have only $1,640 in your account. Good fellow that he is, he deposits $361 to your account. Now you have $2,001. Immediately, he cashes your $2,000 marker.

Now you have one dollar in your account!

There were top Hollywood producers and writers who owed sums like $50,000 and $75,000 and told the casinos they wouldn't pay.

Something had to be done. And so the Nevada legis-lature, under pressure from the owners, passed a bill which, in theory at least, makes all checks and casino debts legal obligations in Nevada.

Each marker is considered an individual obligation and, if not paid, must be deposited against your bank account on the following schedule:

INDIVIDUAL MARKER AMOUNT

$5,000 or less   Within 45 days of the date your marker is accepted by the casino.

| $5,001 to $50,000 | Within 90 days of the date your marker is accepted by the casino |
| Over $50,000 | Within 120 days of the date your marker is accepted by the casino |

The Nevada law also says that the time starts running when you sign the marker and not when you leave the casino.

When paying off markers at the cashier cage, you can't play Juggle-Juggle. The newest marker rather than the oldest is considered as being due first. Thus the older marker moves closer to the time when it must, under the new law, be deposited against your bank account.

Nor will Nevada casinos accept postdated checks.

The trouble with all this, of course, is that Nevada law doesn't prevail in other states. There was a case where a casino sought a $5,000 judgment in Kentucky. It was an open-and-shut case. The casino had the man's check. The defendant had no defense. He didn't even bother to show up on the day the case was to be heard in court.

To everyone's surprise, the judge declared that the debt was invalid. "Casino gambling is not legal in this state. It's a crime. I will, therefore, not allow this court to be used to collect a debt which, if it had been incurred within this state's borders, would be evidence of the commission of a crime."

Public Law 95-109 (the Fair Debt Collection Act) was amended in 1977. It makes it a federal offense for debt collectors to threaten consumers with violence, use obscene language, or contact debtors by telephone at certain inconvenient times or places. Other provisions prohibit debt collectors from publishing "shame" lists, impersonating government officials or attorneys, or collecting more than is legally owed.

How do you avoid owing them money?

1. *Don't* establish credit lines in casinos.
2. *Don't* cash checks in casinos.
3. *Do* carry with you only that amount of cash that you're willing to risk.
4. When you decide how much that is, take a quarter or a third of that and toss it into your bedroom bureau drawer before you leave your home.

You'll thank me for this advice. Because the reality is that if you're out to win, you can do it with a modest stake. If you bring all the ammunition (cash) you can muster, you should ask yourself if you truly want to win.

Does New Jersey collect all of its markers? The casinos like to give you that impression, but it isn't so. Every month large sums are written off by each casino for uncollectible markers.

In 1996, for example, twelve Atlantic City casinos wrote off a total of $24,245,890 in what they label "uncollectible patrons' checks."

But, of course, you want to pay your gaming debts. The trick isn't to avoid paying them, but rather to avoid incurring them.

Keeping Scorecards

When I wrote a chapter in my original book on scoring, I didn't foresee that I was creating a worldwide baccarat-pit change.

At that time, when you asked for a scorecard, you were given one together with a pencil. The pencil was often one of those three-inch stubbies.

Would that I could have patented my scoring creation and collected a royalty for each of those hundreds of thousands of bicolored pens and pencils the casinos have distributed since I published my scoring system! You'll understand the need for them when I tell you how I score.

You want to win at baccarat?
You need a strategy. You, and only you, can decide

how much money you will risk, how much money you want to win, and how long you will play.

Money and time management are the keys that will open the doors to the winner's room.

When I play baccarat, I often limit each of my ventures to two complete shoes. Interestingly enough, and because I'm not in harmony with what's happening on balance, I tend to lose when I sit down and play partial shoes. I've learned that for me, at least, it pays to be patient.

Let's talk about scoring. As a book publisher, I attend the annual Frankfurt Book Fair in Germany. At least once every fair since 1960, I've slipped away for at least an afternoon. I taxi or take a casino bus to the casino at either Bad Homburg or Wiesbaden.

Ancient men and women sit at the roulette tables keeping score. Some manage intricate graphs and charts. The sight of them used to amuse me. Roulette wheels have no memory. Why keep records?

I've learned why in baccarat.

Today I never sit at a baccarat table without first requesting a scorecard. The scorecard (called *Table de Banque* even by dealers who don't speak another word of French) is free for the asking.

My scorecards talk to me. Sometimes they sing to me. Sometimes they whisper words of caution to me. The scorecard tells me things about what's happening that are helpful to know. It alerts me to patterns, trends, and possibilities.

---→

A fantastic shoe for me since I won 44 and lost only 24. This shoe had several streaks and ended with an "unnatural" 40 Player wins to 31 for Bank.

CAESARS PALACE
BACCARAT GAME

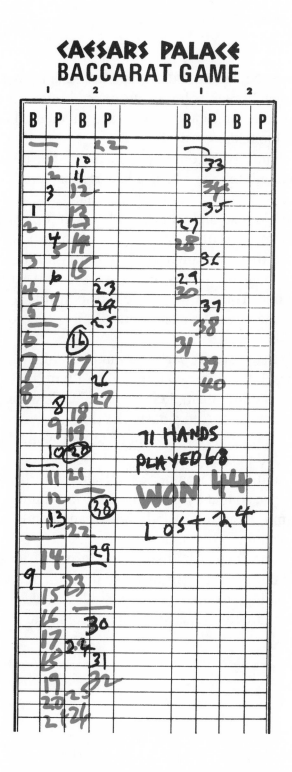

In the beginning, I did what most Asians do. I marked Bank or Player columns with Xs. (Asians have their own scorecards and their own special method for charting table results.)

Columns of Xs didn't tell me much. For instance, the card didn't tell me which side was ahead until I counted every X. It didn't tell me which hands I'd won, which hands I'd lost, and which hands I hadn't played.

My method of keeping score is now so universally copied that I no longer have to carry a red pen and a black pen to casinos; every casino will supply you with one. Yours truly is solely responsible for the fact that today every baccarat pit offers two-color pens or pencils.

On the previous page is a sample card.

I track the decisions: red when I win; black when I lose. I number them. I circle those hands where I didn't make a wager. And a dash like this —— means a Tie.

If I happened to have bet Tie and won, that Tie is recorded in red.

In addition, I number each Bank and Player win in sequence so that by glancing at the last number on each column, I can tell exactly how many hands each side has won up to that moment.

At one time, I had someone in my office tabulate hundreds of cards. He analyzed them for several different findings for me.

Here are the sequences for 160 complete shoes that I played.

Sequence	Bank	Player	Total	Total Hands
1 time	1506	1532	3038	3038
2 times	699	712	1411	2822
3 times	348	376	724	2172
4 times	179	152	331	1324
5 times	94	80	174	870
6 times	48	48	96	576
7 times	29	23	52	364
8 times	7	9	16	128
9 times	3	5	8	72
10 times	2	2	4	40
11 times	1	2	3	33
15 times	1	1	2	30
	2917	2942	5859	11469

If you study the columns, you'll observe that a two-time sequence occurs about half as many times as a sequence of one. A three-timer, half as many as two. A four-timer, half as many as three.

"But this is hindsight!" you may say. "How can it help me?"

It has helped me win thousands upon thousands of dollars. I could fill the pages of an entire book with anecdotes about how.

To cite one example: although aberrations are possible, you now know that a sequence of one usually happens twice as many times as a sequence of two.

One afternoon, I stared at the scorecard in front of me. It was trying to tell me something.

"No bet," I said to the dealer. And for the next two hands, I studied my scorecard.

Although thirty-five hands had been played, there was not a single sequence of one!

From then on, I sat out the deals until the other side won. Then I played the side that had just lost.

I won eight out of the next ten wagers—all chop-chop wins!

It pays to know what's happening. In this case, it paid me more than $11,000 after the so-called "commissions."

I have watched a player bet $30,000 a hand on Bank when my card showed that Player side had so far won thirty-seven hands against twenty-two for the Bank. It was obviously a Player's shoe.

That big-money gambler hadn't learned to "go with the flow."

I have also observed that some people bet one side exclusively. They are rigid Bank bettors or rigid Player bettors.

There is nothing wrong with that except that it has its own built-in Karma. The house percentage will remove money from your pockets with a determination matched only by an Internal Revenue agent.

What did I learn from a further breakdown of several hundred shoes? Well, for one thing—and a thing for which there is no sound or logical explanation—I found that Player comes up more often on both the first and final hands of a shoe.

Why should this be?

There is no logical reason for it. But several times in

heated games, I've remembered that little fact, and more often than not, this aberration repeated itself.

There was also the strange phenomenon that Ties repeated more often than statistics should allow. Again, an aberration, but I've often bet a Tie after a Tie, and I've won more often than the once-in-twelve-and-one-half hands percentages say I should.

Keep a scorecard. Maybe it won't do a thing for you because you have your own peculiar style of betting. But, as the late George Burns used to say, "It can't hurt."

A Postscript on Lady Luck

Author Mario Puzo had a devastating casino experience. He was in London, and there were several hours to kill before his plane took off from Heathrow Airport. He and his lady companion taxied to the casino at the Hilton Hotel.

The dealers were shuffling cards for a new baccarat shoe. He was recognized as the man who wrote *The Godfather*, and he reserved seat #1, which had been vacant. While the cards were being mixed, he wandered to a nearby roulette table where he won a few bets and then quickly lost back the winnings.

Annoyed, he became more involved.

He was summoned, but sent word to "hold the shoe for a minute."

Mario may have written *The Godfather*, but he isn't

one. So a few minutes later, the supervisor at the baccarat game decided not to wait any longer. The shoe with its newly shuffled eight decks was given to the man in seat #2.

When Mario returned to the table, the man in seat #2 had already made eight passes. This was the hand Mario would have dealt. Stunned, he glumly sat down and began to bet—but the size of the bets was modest. Mario likes to bet big on Bank when he deals.

The man went on to make a total of seventeen passes. *Seventeen winning hands for the Bank side!*

The man who had been dealing turned to face Mario. "I wish my wife were here," he said. "I've waited two years for something like this to happen."

"Two years?" Mario snorted. "I've waited all my life for something like this!"

He told me the story on the phone a few days later. "It's enough to make me consider giving up gambling!"

If only he'd returned to the baccarat table a few minutes sooner.

"If only—"

When you are at the baccarat table, observe how many players bet heavier when they are dealing from the shoe. This, as if some force gives them magic powers when they deal the cards.

I do it myself.

And yet reason and logic tell us that the same cards will emerge from the shoe in the identical sequence no matter who deals them out. But that is reason and logic, commodities not present in abundance in gaming halls.

"If only . . ." may be the saddest words you'll hear in

a casino. Even sadder than "Listen, honey, give me that money I told you not to give me."

Life is full of "if onlys," and the casino is life intensified. If only you'd played the slot machine across the aisle. If only you'd bet on red instead of black.

The only "if only" I don't easily forgive because I hear it too often is "If only I'd left the table sooner. . . ."

My own most recent "if only" experience took place this year. I was at Trump Castle in Atlantic City for a weekend. To relax between craps shooting and baccarat, I played a $5 video poker machine.

It seemed to pay off beautifully. Again and again I would win $2,000. And each time I endured the long wait while employees checked the machine, and a W-2 form was issued. (Yes, if you win $1,200 or more at any machine, the casino is obligated to report your win to the IRS.)

I wasn't doing very well at dice or cards. At dinner, I remarked to my wife that I was really enjoying that video poker machine. And I was aiming for the big one, the royal flush that paid $100,000. (I'd won one of these on the cruise ship *Crystal Harmony*. It paid $20,000, and I was told I was the first person to hit a royal flush in the six years of the machine's existence!)

After dinner, instead of returning to the baccarat pit, I headed straight for the $5 poker machine.

Someone else was playing it. But he was waiting, for he had hit an $1,150 combination.

"They really make you wait for your money," I said.

"Yeah," he said, "but I'm willing to wait. An hour ago, I hit the royal for one hundred big ones!"

I managed not to show my bittersweet disappointment and congratulated him. But in my heart of hearts, I was saying to myself, "If only . . ."

The Fell Clutch of Circumstance

We were sitting in the Las Vegas Riviera hotel restaurant having breakfast. I counted out forty $100 bills and handed them to my wife.

"Carole, my love," I said, "take this money. Go directly to the baccarat table, and bet it on Player."

Carole started to protest.

"Hurry!" I said. "You're wasting precious time!"

She strode out, clutching the wad of bills in her fist.

When she returned ten minutes later, she carried her pocketbook, but there was no money in her hand.

"Give it to me!" I commanded. "Eight thousand dollars, please!"

She laughed as she opened her purse to take out the money.

"How did you know?" she asked.

"Because when you came back, your walk was too energetic to reflect disappointment and also because you took so long. It was long enough for me to figure that you had to wait to cash in the chips."

She then recounted what had happened. She'd hurried up to the table and called "$4,000 on Player" just as the cards were about to be dealt.

"You have a bet!" said the supervisor.

It turned out that the man holding the shoe had already dealt five Bank passes and was looking for his sixth. Now he dealt a picture and a 9 to Player and two 4s to himself.

"Player wins 9 over 8."

Carole said people at the table glared at her. It was as if, by breaking in to make her bet, she had somehow changed the sequence of the cards. Nonsense, of course.

And yet, if she hadn't first argued with me, or if she'd walked a little slower, or if I'd gotten the notion a couple of minutes earlier, I'd be minus $4,000 instead of plus $4,000.

I played this little game with my daughter, Sandra Lee, four times with $2,000 bets. She won every time. I did it twice with my friend, Arnold Bruce Levy. He won both times.

What does it mean?

It means that I was lucky. It means that the slightest twist of circumstance could have changed the result. For example, arriving at the table a minute earlier or two minutes later.

Many years ago, I had to wait for a dinner table at a casino's gourmet restaurant. I was assured that the wait would be no more that ten minutes while they set up the table for us.

That delay cost me $30,000.

On another occasion, I was driving back to the MGM Grand, and I couldn't shake a persistent vision of a blackjack hand. I play blackjack only occasionally, but when I stepped into that casino, I couldn't resist taking the involved path to those blackjack tables that allowed $10,000 maximum bets. I called for a $20,000 marker, and as soon as I received the chips, I bet $10,000.

I won the hand, but I was disappointed. You see, I'd had this strong premonition. . . .

Again I bet $10,000.

My next *two* hands were blackjacks!

Three winning hands in a row. Total win: $40,000. Total time spent: ten minutes waiting for the chips and less than five minutes playing.

If I'd arrived a deal or two earlier or later, the results would, of course, have been different.

I play a different style game when I'm ahead than when I'm behind.

I play a different style game when I've had lots of rest and am energy charged.

I play a different style game when I'm feeling good. So will you.

Part of whatever success I've had at the gaming tables is the result of keen insight into how I feel and understanding my deep-down attitudes and energy levels.

As I've mentioned, when I play baccarat, I usually limit myself to two full shoes. But if a cigarette smoker sits next to me (I consider all cigarette smokers suicidal losers) or if I become annoyed by something that happens or by the conduct of another player or a dealer, I summon up the discipline to get up and walk away.

Discomfort is a destroyer. Unhappiness works for the casino. And the casino has enough going for it without those two additional allies.

Tournaments [1]

Some people believe that the million-dollar progressive slot machine is the most exciting new thing that's happened in casinos in a decade.

I happen to think it's the tournament.

Tournaments were obviously designed to draw good customers.

I will report to you on six. Three were baccarat tournaments. I'll include one attempt at a craps championship just to show you the nutty possibilities of human behavior.

Let's start with dice.

I learned that Park Place in Atlantic City was sponsoring a Bally's First Invitational Billy Weinberger Craps Tournament. Weinberger, now dead and mostly forgotten, was then a widely liked and colorful president of the casino. I got to know him when he managed Caesars Palace in Vegas.

The tournament was scheduled for the weekend of May 14.

To enter, you paid a $250 fee. Then you needed $2,000 for the buy-in. I don't embrace the entry-fee concept but, alas, in the early tournaments, it was common. Some casinos figured that the entry fee would add up to the prizes as well as the cost of gifts, overhead, advertising, and promotion. When tournaments were introduced, in some cases an outside organization would be hired to conduct the whole thing and took a fee for doing so.

At any rate, this tournament appealed to me because it was obvious that they'd learned from another casino's fiasco and would avoid allowing partners at the same table.

The partner thing was a big impediment. Today it is rare. (I'll give you an instance later of how it worked.)

Today, too, the casino invariably waives the entry fee for high rollers like myself. I haven't been asked to pay one for a decade, except in the million-dollar tournaments where it costs $10,000 to enter.

Table positions and starting times for the Park Place craps tournament were drawn from a glass fishbowl, thus reducing chances of players "working" with each other.

Play would be for an hour, at which point it would continue only until the shooter made his point or sevened out.

There is an Achilles heel here, for if someone was far

ahead, he could stall the game by getting into petty arguments with the dealers. I prefer a specific number of rolls of the dice, as I prefer a specific number of hands in baccarat tournaments.

The tournament began on a Saturday. I drove to Atlantic City only to be told by a young woman in the glass-walled tournament-office kiosk in the main lobby that this was an "invitational tournament" limited to 250 players. I wasn't invited, and the register of players was full.

I persisted. "Surely there will be some no-shows?"

The young lady phoned a management executive.

"A Mr. Stuart would like to play, but he isn't registered."

"Tell him the rolls are closed."

She told me.

"Ask whomever you're talking with if he believes all those customers will show up."

I heard the voice ask, "Which Mr. Stuart?"

"What's your first name?" she asked.

"Lyle."

"Put him in," the voice instructed.

This was one time when my notoriety helped. New problem: the hotel was packed. When I drove up, I had overheard the doorman tell a parking valet someone had offered him fifty dollars for a room.

Again, a phone call to casino management. I was given a suite.

"Room, food, and beverages are complimentary," the clerk said, after putting my name into his computer.

"Oh, that's nice," I said. Since I'd never gambled at

Bally's Park Place, I asked, "Are they doing that for all tournament players?"

"No sir! It's just that with your level of play—"

That Billy Weinberger was a pretty clever fellow.

I picked a slip from the bowl. I was scheduled to play late that afternoon.

I had no trouble winning at my table.

But I faced a special problem. A couple of months earlier, I'd taken more than thirty employees of our publishing house on a one-week, all-expense-paid vacation in Cuba. We'd had a glorious time. Now the Institute for Cuban Studies was throwing a fund-raising Cuban dinner in a church on Central Park West in Manhattan, and I'd invited twenty-four guests from among those who'd been with me in Havana.

The dinner was scheduled for that Saturday evening.

I pulled a slip from the bowl for the next level of play. Ten P.M.

"I can't make it," I said.

"Sir?"

"I'm taking twenty-four people to dinner in Manhattan in a few hours. The dinner begins at eight."

Consternation. Many phone calls. Finally I was told that one of the casino young ladies would draw slips from the bowl until she picked a Sunday morning position for me. She did.

I drove to New York. I took the crowd to dinner. Hosting was exhausting.

The next morning, accompanied by Carole, I drove back to Atlantic City for the semifinals.

I was zonked out, so it was zombie time. At the craps

table, I reverted to playing against the casino rather than playing against the other players. In my weariness, I lost sight of the goal. I lost.

Carole and I decided to stay to watch the finals.

Each of twelve finalists was given $5,000 in chips. They could cash these in and not play at all. Or they could compete for a first prize of $100,000.

Now, why am I going into such detail on a tournament that has nothing to do with baccarat? Because what followed is identical to what I've seen again and again in baccarat tournaments.

Let me share with you what I've learned about tournaments. In tournaments, you must change your focus. Not everyone can do it. The objective is different. It's no longer a battle against the house. It's *you against the other players*.

Some tournament players can't grasp this.

My strategy for winning is two-fold:

(1) survive;

(2) win enough to double or nearly double your buy-in. (If you do this, you almost certainly have it made.)

Carole and I managed to get table-side positions to watch the roped-off final session through the reflection in a specially installed mirror that hung from the ceiling.

One young man stood out. He wore a necktie and a preppy-style jacket, while the others were all in shirt-sleeves or light sweaters.

The preppy was mostly betting on the "Don't Pass" line and making a series of graduated wagers.

We watched. Even though we weren't personally

involved, Carole later described it as one of the most exciting tournaments she'd ever witnessed.

The announcement came over a loudspeaker. There was one half-hour left to play.

Then: "Twenty minutes left to play."

I counted the preppy's chips. He had more than $13,500 in his rack.

"He *has* it!" I whispered to Carole. "Now if he makes the right move, he has the $100,000 locked up!"

He made the right move!

He bet the required minimum of $100 on the shooter.

Nobody was anywhere close to him in chips.

"Fifteen minutes left to play."

It would be melodramatic to report that the next move he made "horrified" me. Let's just say that it startled and shocked me.

We could see him from his waist to his collar and tie, but we couldn't see his face. I watched him reach for his purple ($500) chips and place two of them on the "Don't Pass" line.

"Why?" I asked myself. "*Why?*"

The shooter threw a four. Our preppy then placed four more purple chips on the table. He was laying two thousand dollars' worth of odds against the four.

The shooter threw lots of numbers. Each time he didn't throw a four, we watched our preppy clap his hands in obvious delight.

Number after number was rolled with no decision.

Then the shooter made his four. The hard way.

"Ten minutes to play," said the announcer over the loudspeaker. I muttered to Carole, "He still has more than $10,000 in chips. He can win if only he holds onto it."

Zilch!

Before the announcement "Five minutes left to play," our preppy had tapped out and quietly slipped away from the table.

Five minutes later, the bell rang signaling the end of the tournament. The last shooter continued to roll the dice. He rolled and he rolled and he made himself a score. His final total was $9,300, and that won the tournament and the $100,000 prize.

Our preppy has to go through the rest of his life knowing that he threw away $100,000 in five foolish minutes.

People do crazy things at tournaments. Shortly I'll tell you about the time I did one myself.

Tournaments [2]

The first baccarat tournament in history took place at the Desert Inn. I believe the prizes were modest—something like a $5,000 first prize.

Baccarat at the D.I. is where one of the famed Dolly Sisters is reported to have sat, played, and lost money every evening for weeks at a time. She loved the game.

The second tournament that I'm familiar with took place at the Tropicana in Las Vegas. It was directed by Norman Luoni.

Luoni was a veteran casino executive. His story was typical of the old days. He had arrived in Las Vegas three decades earlier with just enough money for a motel room and a week's food. He got a job as a security guard. Eventually he became a baccarat dealer, and on the good days, his salary and tokes gave him $100 a day. He became a floorman. He had a keen mind and understood and enjoyed the casino atmosphere.

I learned about this tournament accidentally and alerted myself to watch for the repeat. Nine months later, a second annual tournament was scheduled.

By this time "Pretty Mitzi" Briggs (who had inherited $44 million from her grandfather, the founder of the Stauffer Chemical Company) was out, and Ramada Inns owned the Tropicana. By this time, too, Norm Luoni was working at another casino. And Mitzi Briggs had been separated from all of her $44-million inheritance and was working as a cocktail waitress, where, she announced, "For the first time in my life, I'm truly happy!"

The Tropicana did it the right way. Two hundred thousand dollars' worth of prizes and no entry fee.

The buy-in was $10,000. That means you had to buy $10,000 worth of chips to enter. You had to make a minimum bet of $100 on every hand, and eighty hands would be played.

Whatever money you won or whatever chips you had left when the eighty hands had been played were, of course, yours. You cashed them in. (You *had* to cash them in, for they were special tournament chips, not good for play at any other table game in the casino.)

The first prize was $120,000 and a large silver cup. Second and third prizes were $40,000 and $25,000 respectively. There was a $15,000 fourth prize.

The maximum wager on any hand would be $8,000.

There would be twelve players to a table. The three from each table who had the most money at the end of two shoes would be declared winners and would advance to the finals.

Before flying to Las Vegas, I did my homework. For one thing, I telephoned Norman Luoni from New York.

"Norm," I said, "tell me how it went at the Tropicana's first tournament."

"Well," he said on reflection, "I was surprised. When some players got ahead, I expected the others would make large catch-up bets. Instead, they just sat there like dummies. It's as if they were watching a horse race rather than running in one."

He also told me the interesting fact that the first-prize winner had been a Mexican who, within the first few hands, lost a bold bet of $8,000 (leaving him with less than $2,000), but nevertheless managed to come back and win.

"Did he double the stake? Did he finish with more than $20,000?" I asked.

"Less," Luoni told me.

That gave me the first clue (later reinforced by experience and observation) to the statement I made earlier: if you almost double your buy-in, you've got a fair chance of winning.

I attended the cocktail reception in the Tropicana ballroom on the evening before the tournament. It started late because, I was told, "the plane hasn't arrived yet from Mexico City."

At this point, I didn't know that of the sixty-four players entered in the tournaments, fifty-nine were Mexicans!

The drinks flowed, and the refreshments were lavish.

There were huge spreads of oysters, giant shrimp, crab legs, etc.

Finally, a tournament director pulled names from a hat, and we were each assigned a time and table position.

I was on what they called "the second flight."

While we waited for the first round to start, one of the only four other Americans in the tournament introduced himself.

"You're Lyle Stuart, aren't you?"

"Yes."

"I just wanted to tell you that I love your book. I keep rereading it all the time to remind myself of what gambling in casinos is all about. You've helped me tremendously, and I want to thank you."

After that nice speech, we were both relieved to learn that we weren't assigned the same table and wouldn't be competing against each other.

The first round began. Within minutes a dapper, diminutive, bespectacled man had $40,000 in front of him.

I assumed that he would be the winner.

Never assume anything in gambling. Ten minutes later, he was back to less than his original $10,000 stake.

Minutes later, he was up again to $25,000.

Before the thirtieth hand, he tapped out.

I was told that he then hurried to the regular baccarat table and dropped $60,000.

He hadn't learned the prime rule of tournament play: you don't play to win house money. Your only goal is to end up with more chips than anyone else at the table.

It was my time to play. At the end of seventy hands, I couldn't determine whether I was in second or third place. You had to be one of the top three of the fourteen at the table to qualify for the finals.

My technique was so low-key that one supervisor later remarked at how surprised he was by my stack of chips. I had about $14,000 in front of me.

Then I tumbled into a trap set by inexperience. I decided the players close behind me (there were two of them) would be making big bets to jump ahead of me. I neglected to remember Norm Luoni's observation that you'd expect them to do it, but they don't. To assure second place, I bet $3,000. I lost. I bet another $3,000. I lost.

I was now out of the money.

I had the impulse to wager six or eight thousand dollars on the next hand to make a recovery, but I recognized that I'd lost my cool. I was disconcerted by my two consecutive losses, so I resolved not to continue paying due to my sudden unlucky streak.

Good thing.

I lost the next six (small) bets.

I couldn't do anything right.

I ended up with $8,500 of my $10,000 buy-in.

Four of the twelve players had tapped out.

The two players whose chips I couldn't measure with my eyes and whom I was sure would make large last-minute bets sat frozen. They did nothing.

I didn't make the finals, but I watched them. The last hand. My American fan was in the finals and was neck and neck for third place.

Bets were placed in order of seating. At the other side of the table, two Mexicans, obvious partners, made their wagers. One bet $8,000 on the Bank. One bet $8,000 on Player.

Bank side won. The tournament was over. The two Mexicans shook hands and prepared to receive their silver cups and divide the $160,000 in prizes, plus what they'd won at the table.

It was my first baccarat tournament, and for me, it was full of excitement and pleasure. It made ordinary gambling seem like an electric typewriter as compared to a high-speed word processor.

A short time later, the Tropicana announced another baccarat tournament.

I registered immediately.

I looked forward to the tournament. I had heard from friends in the business that the Tropicana was running unlucky and had suffered losses in eighty out of ninety shifts. The "hold" had dropped from 28 to 29 percent to 16 percent. There was no cheating. No more than the usual hanky-panky by customers and dealers. But the people in charge knew that the situation would right itself with time, and indeed it did.

Then I broke my femur for the second time when I took a fall on a street in Port Maria, Jamaica.

An ambulance rushed me to a hospital in Kingston. I could suffer the pain; I'd been through it all before. But, as I explained to my old friend, the surgeon who'd also operated on me the first time and was about to operate again, there was a tournament I had to enter in one week.

"It can't be done," he told me.

"Not even on a stretcher and using crutches?"

"No way," he said.

I was so sure that I knew so much about tournament play now that I could almost "taste" that first prize!

I wasn't unhappy, therefore, when I had a call from my office telling me that the Tropicana had phoned to say the tournament was canceled. This time, they'd had only four entries. (When the peso began to evaporate in value and few Mexicans would attend, the Tropicana $10,000 buy-in baccarat tournament was given a quiet burial.)

An invitational tournament replaced it. This one required a $2,000 entry fee. Players would be given $25,000 in "play money" chips to compete with. The player holding the most in chips at the end of the final round would receive a first prize of $50,000. Second prize: $10,000. It was a far stretch from the original $200,000-in-prizes Tropicana tournament.

Next I observed but didn't play in a tournament at the Sands in Atlantic City. Came the last hand. The two obvious contenders had exactly $35,000 in front of each of them. Not a dollar more. Not a penny less. One was an American, the other an obvious foreigner.

It was, as the dealers told me later, one of the most exciting moments in gambling that they'd ever watched.

It was the American's turn to bet first. The rules for this tournament had no ceiling on the amount one could wager. He had secret bet slips* left, but decided not to

---

*There was a tradition of giving each player two or three small pieces of paper that were secret bet slips. You could use these anytime to write the amount of

Secret bet card.

use them. He openly pushed his entire $35,000 onto the Bank square.

The other man was a wealthy Iranian. Some people ascribe what happened next to a language-communication problem. He elected to make a secret bet.

Keep in mind that this wasn't necessary. The American had already made his wager and couldn't change it. There was no sense to secrecy.

Now, if the Iranian also pushed *his* $35,000 onto the Bank side and Bank won, he and the American would split the first and second prizes between them. They'd split $310,000 and each take home $155,000. If Bank lost, both men would have been wiped out, and someone else at the table would have been the winner.

If the Iranian had wagered anywhere from $100 to $35,000 on Player side, and Player won, he'd have won $250,000.

As it later turned out, the Iranian wrote on the paper: "Bank $34,000. Tie $1,000."

True, if that one-in-twelve-times Tie had shown up, he'd have won the candy store.

Bank won. The man who'd bet $35,000 won a total of $33,250 on his bet plus the $250,000 first prize.

The Iranian, by making that $1,000 tie wager, won $32,300 on his Bank bet and cut himself to second

---

your wager rather than put the chips on the table. This way other players wouldn't know what side or how much you were betting on a hand until everyone else had placed their bets. This has pretty much been dropped, and in today's tournaments, the only secret bet allowed is the final wager of the shoe.

place in a no-win situation. His prize was $60,000. The $950 differential cost him $190,000!

If you talk to tournament veterans, you'll hear dozens of stories like this.

In the intense excitement of tournament play, you tend to lose more than your money.

Sometimes you lose your head.

Tournaments (3)

It was billed as "The World Championship of Casino Games," and it was held at the Atlantic City Sands Hotel.

Actually, there were four separate tournaments. You could compete in craps, roulette, blackjack, or baccarat. The prizes were $15,000 for each game.

There was no entry fee, and the buy-in was $2,000 for each game. You could enter one tournament, or two, or all of them.

The winner of the most money in each game would receive a $15,000 prize. Then the winners of each of the four contests would be given $5,000 worth of chips to compete against each the winners of the other three games.

As a finalist, you'd have to play all four games. The

player with the most money at the end of the four contests would be "World Champion." His award would be another $25,000 on top of the $15,000 from the original tournament that he'd won. In addition, he could keep the $5,000, plus whatever he won in the final game, plus any other money he'd won along the way.

It was a lovely deal for the player.

The casino hired the D. L. Blair Company to supervise the project.

Thirty-five of *Fortune* magazine's top fifty corporations are Blair clients. Blair oozes integrity and conducts most of those product sweepstakes so widely advertised in newspapers and magazines. They even have a Nebraska town named after them where sweepstakes entries are sent.

I entered the baccarat tournament.

I faced fifty-three competitors. Two of the four tables had fourteen players, and two had thirteen. There would be one winner at each table, and the winners at each of the four tables would play against each other in the finals.

I was the winner at my table.

The starting time for the final round kept being postponed while the Blair people tried to locate the fourth contestant. It seems that they'd inadvertently given him the wrong starting hour.

While they searched, I hung out with the other two finalists. One was a jovial bookmaker from Atlanta, Georgia. He talked the kind of gaming lingo wherein $500 is "a nickel" and $1,000 is "a dime."

The second man was a pleasant middle-aged chap

who, a few hours before, learned that he'd become a grandfather. I decided that because he won at his table with less than his original $2,000 stake, he had "lucked" into the finals.

The missing player was located at last. I learned that he was a recent immigrant from Turkey. He and I were positioned at one end of the table and the other two at the opposite end.

The two players at the far end went into immediate action. They both adopted a tournament strategy that works sometimes. They lunged into the game with large bets. That strategy calls for getting far ahead of the others at the beginning and then coasting to hold the lead.

It contains the risk that you'll be knocked out of the ring before the first round is ended.

The two men at the far end of the table were lucky. Starting with $500 and moving to $1,000 bets, they both increased their stakes to somewhere between $3,000 and $4,000.

The man at my right seemed to be running unlucky. He lost most of his wagers and was soon down to $600. In my mind, I clocked him as a loser.

Early conclusions are not always accurate ones.

I watched him place his last $600 on Bank. He won. He let it all ride. He won again.

Now he had $2,281 after "commissions." In this tournament, the so-called "commission" had to be settled after each hand.

He was back in the game as a contender.

One Blair regulation that we all objected to was the rule that once you were seated, you couldn't stand and walk around the table. Since there was no compensating regulation on how one's chips had to be stacked, you couldn't know clearly how much money the other players had.

We found this frustrating in the preliminary games, so all four of us agreed that, if asked, we'd count our chips and announce where we stood.

Hand sixty. Twenty more to go.

The bookie from Atlanta called over, "Hey, Lyle boy. How much gold you got there?"

I counted carefully. "Thirty-seven hundred and seventy-five," I announced.

"Shee-it! That puts you ahead of me!"

I laughed. "That's where I'm supposed to be!"

He immediately returned to a series of larger bets. His companion at the far end followed suit. I decided to stay where I was.

Three passes for the Player side. The shoe moved across the table to me.

"You're gonna make a big Bank streak," the bookie called as he put $1,000 in the Bank square in front of him. "I'm even bettin' a dime on you!"

Three Player hands in a row. The Rule of Three prevailed here. I placed my wager in the Player box. It was the second time in the shoe that this had happened.

I won the bet and lost the shoe.

I was pleased with myself. I'd followed my Rule of Three. Player had won three hands in a row, and so my philosophy said I had to bet Player—even though I had the shoe and would turn over the Bank's hand.

Hand seventy-two. My shoe. I bet $500 on Bank.

Player won. Player won the next three hands, and soon the shoe was mine again. Except that this time on its journey around the table, both men at the far end had tapped out.

The supervisor from Blair announced, "Hand seventy-six."

Four more hands to go. I was nicely ahead of my Turkish opponent. All I had to do now was to stay solid. I'd match his bets. That way I'd win or lose as much on each hand as he did, and there was no way he could pass me.

He had to make the first wager. He bet $200 on Player.

Remember that Rule of Three that I keep talking about? I, too, could have bet $200 on the Player side.

There were other possibilities. If I felt a strong attraction to Bank, I could have ignored my rule and made a small Bank bet. Then, even if I lost, the $400 swing in his favor wouldn't have altered the fact that I was ahead.

Hand seventy-six. I had a lock on the championship. They could hand me the $15,000 prize money now. It was mine. The other fellow looked to have little more than $1,000 in front of him. No contest. I had almost $4,000 in chips.

I glanced up.

Perhaps 100 spectators stood transfixed on the other side of the rail that separated the baccarat pit from the rest of the casino.

The spectators were scarcely breathing. A Rembrandt oil painting.

And then I did a crazy thing.

Crazy.

I violated all logic and all of my basic rules. The little boy that's in all of us surfaced in me. I was suddenly James Bond. I'd show those spectators something to remember!

I pushed $3,000 onto the Bank square. This left me less than $950, but I was unconcerned.

Did someone in the crowd gasp, or was I just imagining it?

I dealt a natural 9 to the Player.

I dealt myself a 7.

I had blown it.

For several days thereafter, I couldn't face myself.

Months later, when I had that second leg break, my son Rory put aside his jazz guitar in Boulder, Colorado, long enough to fly to Jamaica and sit by my side. He was there after the femur was pinned and I was wheeled from the operating theater back to my hospital bed.

This shoe was a pleasure. I bet $10,000 on the first hand and again on the second. This left me with a net profit of $9,500 and a nice way to begin.

Thereafter, I was more conservative, and my wagers were $1,000 to $3,500.

I played sixty-seven of the seventy-eight hands that resulted in decisions. There were four Ties. I won thirty-seven hands and lost thirty. If you handle money intelligently, it's pretty hard not to make a profit when you win seven more hands than you lose. The winnings from this shoe paid for a cruise on the Crystal Harmany in a first-class cabin.

P	B	P	B	P	B	P	B
	1	(14)			22		30
	2		9		(23)		31
1		—		21			32
(2)		(15)		22		32	
3			10	—			33
4		16		23			(34)
5			(11)	24		33	
6			12	25			35
7			(13)	—			36
	3		14		24		37
	4		15	26		34	
	5		16		25		38
8			17	27			39
	6	17		28		35	
9			18		26	—	
	7	18		29		36	
10			19		27		40
(11)			20	30			41
	8	19		31		37	
(12)			21		28		
(13)		20			(29)		

78 HANDS
PLAYED 67
WON 37
LOST 30   TIES 4

For the balance of the day, I lay heavily sedated by the anesthetic. Rory says I lay there for hours and mumbled nothing but gibberish.

Except once. In a loud, clear voice, I suddenly exclaimed, "Just four more hands and I had it!"

I still hadn't forgiven myself.

Postscript on A Fool at Play

My Turkish competitor dealt the last three hands. They were all won by the Bank side.

He went on to play against the winners of the three other tournaments.

Two finalists lost all of their chips on the first three games.

Blackjack was the last of the four games to compete in. The Turk sat at the blackjack table, playing against the only contestant remaining. It was the last of the four games. He needed to win this one for the championship and another $25,000.

His opponent was an investment stock adviser who happened to be of Greek ancestry. Thus it was Turk against Greek! (Years before, I'd written a humorous song with orchestra leader Joseph Cherniavsky, titled

"Talking Turkey to a Greek." It didn't make the Hit Parade.)

Came the final hand: the eightieth.

The Turk was comfortably ahead. The Greek was at an obvious disadvantage because the marker had moved back and forth, and now it was his turn to be first. The Turk simply had to match any bet the Greek made.

For all practical purposes, the game was over.

The Greek, knowing that he couldn't win, made the required minimum $100 bet.

My madness may have been contagious. The Turk pushed out $2,000 in chips as his bet.

The dealer showed the jack of clubs as his open card. He gave each player a total of 19. Then he turned over his hole card: an ace. Blackjack!

Just as I gave a tournament crown to the Turk, so did the Turk hand the championship to the Greek, along with the $25,000 additional prize money.

And that's how Xen Angelidis, a lovely man and one of my neighbors in Fort Lee, New Jersey, became the first World Champion of Gambling.

Tournaments [4]

The *New York Post* blew the cover on three roommates who managed to win $186,000 in Atlantic City tournaments within a five-week period. They divided their winnings four ways, although one of their quartet had yet to win a tournament.

For history, let me record their names: David Warling, David Gatenby, Michael Meyer, and John Lertola.

Were these seasoned casino gamblers? Not at all. Three were all of twenty-four years old, and one was twenty-nine. They all worked for Bell Laboratories in Holmdel, New Jersey. They were computer engineers.

What they did was simple enough. When two managed to get assigned to the same table, they would play on opposite sides, and they would bet minimum $5 bets.

Then, at the appointed moment, usually the last hand in the game, they would each bet their entire bankrolls on opposite sides.

They learned with their computers what I've already passed on to you. If you end up with a bankroll almost twice the size of your buy-in, you are a shoo-in.

Immediately after the newspaper article about them, several casinos took steps not to include the four in their invitational tournaments or, if they were entered, to make certain they weren't assigned tables with each other.

The Las Vegas Tropicana held one of its invitational baccarat tournaments. I was invited and decided to enter. I flew west with Carole.

I yearned for the days of old when the casino contributed prizes totaling $200,000. This time, a chunk of the prizes actually came from the players themselves, since each had to pay a $1,000 entry fee. If all 100 registered players showed up, there would be $100,000 in prizes.

As it was, seventy players entered the tournament.

Each player started with $25,000 in nonnegotiable play-money chips.

A contest round would consist of playing one full shoe. The minimum bet was $100 and the maximum, $8,000. Tie bets were permitted, and each player was entitled to two secret wagers.

As I explained earlier, the purpose of secret wagers is to allow the player to spring a surprise on his competitors. For example, if someone is ahead of you and the game is almost over, the leader might match every bet you make on the theory that even if he loses, you have lost, too, and so he continues to remain in the lead. This is called shadowing. The secret bet short-circuits his chance of shadowing for at least two hands.

The Tropicana tournament consisted of three rounds. The three players at each table with the most money at the end of the first game would compete in a semifinal. At the end of this round, the four players with the most money at each table would compete in the finals.

Each finalist was guaranteed a $1,000 prize. (Or, in effect, a return of the entry fee.)

At the time, I did my serious baccarat gambling at Caesars Palace. That's where we "bunked," if you can call it bunking. Our living room had a bar and refrigerator, a giant-screen color TV, and a grand piano. Our bedroom had two Roman-style sunken baths the size of small swimming pools.

The hotel registration clerk mentioned that we also would have a Jacuzzi, but neither Carole nor I could locate it. (Three days later, I opened a door that I'd thought was an extra closet and discovered that our suite had an additional bedroom with bath and, sure enough, a Jacuzzi.)

The first night, I played baccarat at Caesars for twenty minutes or so and walked away $21,000 ahead. I put it into a safe-deposit box in the cashier's cage, thus practicing what I preach in my *Winning at Casino Gambling* book ($18 at bookshops everywhere!).

Carole and I then taxied to the Tropicana where we attended the cocktail party and dinner buffet for tournament players. Table positions were selected by drawing slips of paper from a hat. Then a casino executive explained the rules of the tournament.

Just before we walked into the ballroom, I surprised Carole by unexpectedly entering her in the tournament.

After dinner, I outlined a strategy for her to follow. Then we returned to the Palace for a Barry Manilow concert. (I can understand the appeal of Keno, slot machines, Pow Gai, and the Big Six wheel, but I doubt that I'll ever understand the appeal of Barry Manilow.)

The strategy I outlined for Carole? Keeping in mind that in most tournaments, several players are tapped out by the end of the game, one goal is to last out the shoe.

I suggested that she make a substantial bet on the first hand. If she won, great! She'd be in the lead and could rest on her laurels with minimum bets. (In this case, $100 was the minimum bet.)

If she lost, it would make no difference: then she would stay with the minimum allowable bet.

Since there are almost eighty hands in a shoe, you do this for the first fifty-five or sixty hands. Once in a while, if you have a strong hunch, make a strong bet. But mostly, stay with the minimums.

Then you look around. When it came to the last eight to ten hands left in the shoe, supervisory personnel would count and announce the assets of all remaining players.

Now you make your move. You make bold wagers in an effort to jump out into the first-place position.

It isn't a bad strategy. It has worked often, which is all you can ask of any casino-gaming strategy.

Carole and I were assigned to separate tables. We were both among the top three at our respective tables, and thus we qualified for the semifinals.

Again we were at separate tables. This time I made an $8,000 first wager on the Player side. Bank won.

When we were a few hands from the end, I made my move. I had frivolously used up my two secret bets. A fellow to my right knew that I was close to moving ahead of him, so he shadowed my wagers, chip for chip.

He ran into only one problem: I lost wager after wager, and so did he.

When the chips were counted, he had fallen behind another player at the far end of the table, and we both lost our chance to compete in the final round.

Carole won at her table.

She would be in the finals. (That is, if anxiety didn't fell her first!)

This meant staying on in Las Vegas until Monday. It meant delaying our return flight to New York by a day. And, alas, it meant staying in casinos too long for my personal gaming philosophy.

I began to lose money at the other games.

The time arrived for the finals.

Again Carole and I discussed strategy. I reminded her that she was playing with play money, and it wouldn't reflect any glory for her to have lots of chips in front of her at the end of the shoe unless she was a winner.

Since first prize was $50,000 and second, a comparatively small $10,000, she would go for all or nothing: win first prize.

I assured her that she could do it.

The rules did not allow spectators to talk to the

players. But nowhere was it written that I couldn't talk to a fan of mine who stood next to me, as we both stood at the rope behind Carole. He was an avid reader of my book who had recognized me and had observed my every move in the semifinals.

"If you'd won that first wager, you'd have won," he sagely observed.

Just then Carole made her $8,000 first wager. She lost.

She reverted to the $100 minimum bets.

She was aware that she was now competing against more-sophisticated punters than she'd faced in the first two rounds.

Nevertheless, by the sixtieth hand, four players tapped out and left the table. Charles Bazarian of Oklahoma, trying deliberately to act obnoxious so as to upset the other players, shouted and chomped on his unlit cigar. He ran into a streak of losing bets. Finally, he placed his remaining chips on Bank. Suddenly he was on a winning streak.

At countdown time, Carole was fourth.

Bazarian now had more than $50,000 worth of chips in front of him. But his discipline had begun to erode, and instead of holding his lead, he continued to make large bets and lost several of them.

I said to my spectator companion within Carole's earshot, "What she has to do when the shoe reaches her is to make a big bet."

Bazarian had allowed his $50,000 to shrink to $30,000.

Carole had worked her bankroll up to about $18,000.

She needed a few big wins.

I watched her write a secret bet. (*Why* she decided to make a secret bet, we'll never know, since nobody was chasing or matching her.)

The shoe moved to Carole.

She dealt.

Bank won.

I was pleased. "I'll bet she wagered $8,000," I said loudly to my companion, watching the back of her head.

Carole nodded yes.

"I'll bet she wagered on herself—on the Bank side."

Carole shook her head no.

Her secret bet, designed to deceive everyone at the table, was $8,000 on Player side. (It sure fooled me!)

She lost the bet, but kept the shoe. But the effect of the $16,000 swing was all too clear. It destroyed her will to win.

The $16,000 funny-money disadvantage ended her chances at the real-money first prize of $50,000. Had she bet on Bank, it would have taken another bet or two to jump ahead of the number one player.

Now she reverted to wagers of a few hundred dollars, losing sight of the fact that nothing mattered except to come in ahead of all the others, which is what Charles Bazarian did.

Still, as a tournament, it was exciting and it was fun.

Postscript: that evening we went downtown. Ash Resnick, a mob-connected employee of Steve Wynn, spotted me across the crowded casino floor.

I told him for the first time how, several years before, his legendary rival, casino owner Sandy Waterman, had lunched with me and asked me to join him in investing in a projected Atlantic City casino.

Sandy had sat unnoticed in the Café Roma of Caesars Palace—a casino where he had been chief honcho less than a year earlier. He remarked to me, "Do you know, if I knew I had only two weeks to live, I'd kill Ash Resnick."

Six days later, Sandy dropped dead of a heart attack.

Ash said that Waterman had been angry at him, but insisted that the anger was misdirected and without justification.

He also insisted that Carole and I be driven back to Caesars Palace in one of Steve Wynn's stretch limousines.

By departure time the next morning, I was down $71,000.

I had stayed at the fair too long.

I arranged for Xen Angelidis to taxi with us to the airport. We were scheduled to meet him at the hotel entrance.

Carole and I walked through the casino on the way to our suite to prepare to check out.

"Go upstairs, and I'll join you there," I told her. "I want to play a little baccarat."

"Do we have time?"

"We've got about twenty minutes. I'll be right up. I promise."

I hurried to the baccarat pit where I had them check the computer to confirm my own memory. Caesars

Palace was holding $44,000 worth of my markers. I only had $6,000 remaining on my $50,000 credit line.

"Give me the six," I said.

There was only a hand or two left in the shoe. I waited for a new shoe, meanwhile glancing at my wristwatch.

As luck would have it, there were several Asians at my table who had that habit of peeking at the cards by grasping the top and rolling them over slowly. Eight new decks had to be opened, checked, and shuffled.

This time, mixing the decks seemed to me to take forever.

The shoe was ready at last, and the game began.

I made wagers on six out of the first seven hands. I lost five of my six bets.

The shoe came to me.

I audited my chips. Of my original $6,000, only $3,200 was left.

I remembered Charles Bazarian, the man with the cigar who'd won the $50,000 first prize in the Tropicana tournament and how he'd bet everything he had on one hand, won, and went on into a winning streak.

A shortage of time dictated that I do the same.

I bet the entire $3,200 on Bank. I dealt the shoe. I won.

I let the $6,400 sit on the Bank side. I won again.

I bet $7,500 and made a $100 bet for the dealers. I dealt myself another winning Bank hand.

I bet $10,000. I won.

I won four more passes of $10,000 each.

I lost the next bet. $10,000.

I'd had the shoe for no more than five minutes.

I was ahead more than $50,000 for the session.

I raced to the casino cashier cage to redeem markers.

Up to the room and then down to the hotel cashier to check out and pay my incidentals.*

The lady behind the counter told me I had a hotel bill of $2,400.

"I think you're mistaken," I said. "I'm comped."

"It doesn't say that here," she said.

"I'm sorry, but I'm in a hurry. Please check with the casino."

One quick phone call, and the bill was canceled.

I raced down the hotel steps just as the bellman came along with our luggage.

"I made a good recovery," I told Carole, as I got into the back of the cab.

"How much?"

"Enough so that my net loss is less than $17,000."

I thought I caught a smirk on her face. I was right. She revealed that *she* was leaving Las Vegas a $7,000 *winner*!

"Maybe *I* should write the book on how to win at baccarat," she said.

On the other hand, having turned a $71,000 loss into a less-than-$17,000-loss, I felt like something of a winner, too!

---

*For the uninitiated, "incidentals" consist of phone calls, dry cleaning and laundry charges, and tips added to room-service bills. In other words, any cash outlays that the casino has to pay on your behalf. This sometimes, but not always, includes those pay-to-view movies you order on your TV screen.

I Win My First Tournament

One doesn't hear much about baccarat tournaments in Las Vegas anymore, but they are still played often in Atlantic City.

I decided it was time for me to win one.

I knew a tournament was scheduled at Bally's Grand. First prize $75,000, plus the casino pays the tax.

The trouble was that we were on a vacation trip paid for by the casino. A total of six couples spent a day in Atlantic City and then were taken, each couple in a separate limo, to Philadelphia International Airport. There, we were flown first class to Phoenix. Again, each of the six couples was transported by limousine to the Phonecian Hotel in Scottsdale.

In addition to everything being comped, Carole was given several hundred dollars worth of gift-buying power at the shops on the premises.

We had a wonderful time. We got to know the others and were all congenial. At the end of six days, we were scheduled to be flown back to New York to be met by a limo which would carry us to Fort Lee.

On the day we spent in Atlantic City, I won $55,000.

I certainly didn't want to get into a situation where I'd lose it back. The knowledge of that tournament haunted me. It was time for me to win one.

We asked to be taken to Atlantic City instead of Fort Lee.

We got there just in time for me to enter the tournament.

Atlantic City baccarat tournaments are usually for three rounds of thirty hands each. Four or five players who win the most chips in the first round move on to the second. Then two or three move into the final.

I had my betting strategy down pat. My tournament play was mostly going to happen in the final ten hands. The first twenty didn't matter. I would make minimum bets, hope other players would tap out, then use my ammunition for the last ten hands.

I easily won the first two rounds.

The final round was tougher. And decision time came down to the last (thirtieth) hand.

On the next-to-the-last deal, chips are counted by the casino, and each player's total is announced.

The only person who could beat me was the fellow on my left. He did a lot of figuring with pencil and paper. If I bet this much on that side, and he bet this much on this side, etc.

When the croupier announced, "This is the last hand.

This is the final hand of the shoe," I did some thinking.

In an ordinary game, sophisticated players often bet Player for the last hand and frequently also bet Tie.

This was not truly the last hand in the shoe. It was the last hand of thirty deals.

Instinct told me that the guy to my left would bet Player. He'd had the shoe and dealt a Player win. The shoe moved to me, and I dealt another Player win.

Now it had moved to the fellow on my right. He had a shot at second place—but only if the guy on my left or I lost a big wager.

Now it was time for the last and secret bet. I bet Bank.

Sure enough, the man to my left made a maximum wager on Player.

Player showed 7.

The fellow with the shoe turned one card face up, 4.

"I need another 4," I said.

He peeked at the hole card.

"Will this do?" he asked with a broad grin. He flipped over a 5 for a winning total of 9.

Thus, on the single flip of a card was a fortune made.

All told, I walked away from that tournament $110,000 richer.

Afterwards, I told Carole that I was thinking of rewriting my baccarat book.

"To do that," she said, "you should win another tournament."

I Win My Second Tournament

Carole has observed that when I dabble without the will to win, I merely go through the motions.

I entered another tournament. This one was played with funny money. You were given $4,000 in worthless chips.

I gave it my best shot and thought I'd be taking home another first prize. By the twenty-ninth hand, I had more than $8,000 and was far ahead of everyone at the semifinal table. Now came the final wager: the secret bet.

I bet just so that no matter what anyone wagered on Bank or Player, I'd remain number one.

I'd overlooked something. Tournaments played with real money allow Tie wagers of $100 to $250. This one allowed $1,000 Tie bets. So, three fellows who were trailing everybody and had nothing to lose, bet $1,000 on Tie.

Tie came in. They were now $9,000 plus, and all three went on to the finals.

It was then that I decided not to play in any tournament where play money is the betting currency. I believed it unlikely that any of the three would have bet $1,000 if it was a thousand of their own real dollars.

I wanted to win a second tournament to validate this book. The Taj Mahal announced one with a $100,000 first prize.

This would consist of three thirty-hand rounds. It would be played with chips equal to real money. It was for me.

The tournament was conducted in the Taj Mahal's poker room. It was oversubscribed. The only feature of this one that I didn't care for was the reentry round. If you were defeated in the first session, you could pay another entry fee and have a second chance to play in a first round contest.

I won the first and second rounds without much trouble.

When they let down the velvet rope to allow finalists into the pit, I was so cocky that I said, "Hold it! Let the winner walk in first!" The other players were startled as I pushed my way past them and sauntered in.

It was obnoxious, and I relate it only to reflect how confident I was.

I did my usual thing. I played minimum $50 bets for the first twenty hands. Then I went into action. My scorecard told me it was a Player shoe, so I tested the water with large ($800) bets.

No one was even close to me by the final round. I won the $100,000 first prize easily.

As I was writing the final chapters to this book, I decided it would be whipped cream on the charlotte russe if I could win a third.

There was one problem. In January 1997, I broke my left leg again. I had just graduated from a walker to crutches. When the Taj Mahal announced a tournament with a $100,000 first prize, I entered. I might have hesitated had I known how exhausting it would be to move around that giant casino* on crutches.

There were 156 contestants. On March 27, the day before Easter Sunday, I had no difficulty being first at my table in round one. Of the fourteen at each table, five moved into the semifinals.

By the twenty-ninth hand in the semifinals, I was the fifth highest chip holder. But since only three persons moved on to the finals, I knew I had to give it everything I had.

When a supervisor announced the amount each player held, I wrote down the numbers. Then I did

---

*In his magazine, *Trump Style*, Trump claims that "at 135,000 square feet, the Taj casino is the largest in the world." Sorry, Donald. Caught you exaggerating again! The MGM Grand has 171,500 square feet. It's the size of four football fields. Nonetheless, waltzing across the Taj casino is enough to exhaust this writer when he's on crutches.

BACCARAT TOURNAMENT

BACCARAT TOURNAMENT

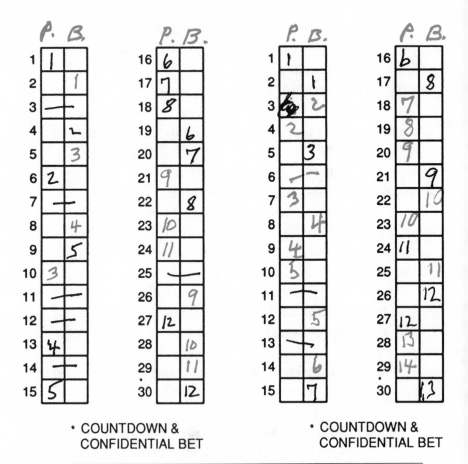

* COUNTDOWN &
  CONFIDENTIAL BET

* COUNTDOWN &
  CONFIDENTIAL BET

Here are the three scorecards that trace the path to winning the $100,000 first prize in the April 15th baccarat tournament at the Taj Mahal. There were 154 entrants. (Had I entered and won the *next* Taj tournament that took place on September 9, 1995, my fitrst prize would have been $150,000.)

FINALS

TRUMP
TAJ MAHAL
CASINO • RESORT ™

BACCARAT
TOURNAMENT

#	P	B		#	P	B
1	1			16		6
2	2			17		7
3	3			18		8
4	4			19	10	
5	5			20	11	
6	6			21	12	
7	7			22	13	
8		1		23		9
9	—			24		10
10		2		25	14	
11	8			26	15	
12		3		27		11
13	9			28		12
14		4		29	16	
15		5		30		13

* COUNTDOWN &
CONFIDENTIAL BET

In round one, I won four hands and lost four hands in the first ten deals. Three out of the next five hands were Ties. Note that I lost seven hands in a row. However, these were minimum $50 or near-minimum $100 wagers.

Only with hand # twenty-one did I get serious.
Then my bets were larger, and I won six and lost two.
Five of the fourteen players advanced to the semifinals. By the twenty-fifth hand, I had become the
largest winner at the table. The fina hand, the "secret
bet," required only a minimum wager because at the
countdown, I saw that nobody could match me even
if they bet and won the maximum—as long as I lost
no more than $50 on the hand.

In the semifinal round, three of the fourteen players at the table advanced to the final round. I won sixteen hands of the twenty-seven that produced
decisions. Again, I was the largest winner at the
table.

Lady Luck truly kissed my brow in the finals. I
won twenty hands and lost only nine. Note that I violated my Rule of Three after Bank won five hands.
My research shows, for no rational reason, that the
sixth hand is the difficult one to win. So I switched
and ran into a series of four Player wins. By the time
I'd won the twenty-nineth hand, no one was even
close to me. Again, my final wager was only $100.
Two months later, the Taj Mahal sponsored a
$1,300,000 invitational tournament with a f'irst prize
of $1,000,000. This one required a $10,000 entry fee.

careful figuring. Four players were ahead of me. If this one bet so much on Bank and I bet Player, what would that do? If that one bet Tie and Tie came in, where would that leave me?

I held up the game for a few minutes after every other player had made secret bets. Finally, I calculated that the three leaders would make small wagers and hope to maintain their positions.

The minimum bet allowed was $100. The maximum, $2,000. One could wager up to $250 on Tie in increments of $25.

After my careful figuring, I bet $1,750 on Player and $200 on Tie.

Player won. I was number one at the table.

I felt pretty confident about winning that $100,000. But I wasn't prepared for the unexpected.

In tournaments, you don't waste anything. I have seen big money lost because someone had $8 more than someone else. For that reason, I stay clear of the Tie bet.

In my first round, I was pleased that players had poured a small fortune into Tie bets and not a single Tie showed up in the thirty hands.

At my semifinal table, only one Tie came up in thirty hands.

Now, as the finals began, there were twelve players. I watched as at least six of them bet Tie on the first hand. "Good," I thought to myself, "they'll dissipate their strength early."

Tie came up on the first hand!

Some got $200 for their $25. A couple had bet $50

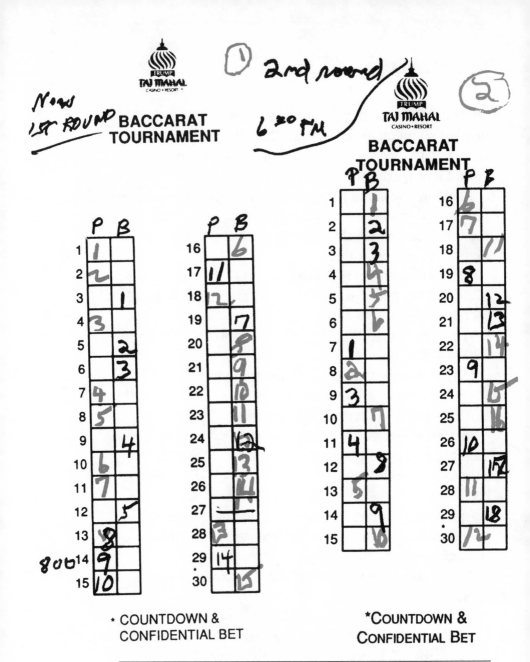

This March 29, 1997, tournament card reflects what is probably the unluckiest streak I've ever run into at a baccarat table. I played only ten hands and lost eight of them!

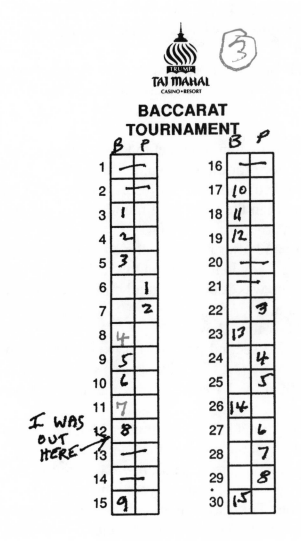

BACCARAT
TOURNAMENT

	B	P			B	P
1	—		16		—	
2	—		17		10	
3	1		18		11	
4	2		19		12	
5	3		20		—	
6		1	21		—	
7		2	22			3
8	4		23		13	
9	5		24			4
10	6		25			5
11	7		26		14	
12	8		27			6
13	—		28			7
14	—		29			8
15	9		30		15	

I WAS OUT HERE →

*COUNTDOWN &
CONFIDENTIAL BET

and were paid $400.

Now almost every player bet the Tie to repeat. I didn't.
It did.

I'd bet Bank in those first two no-decision hands. I
was disheartened to note that while I still had my original $2,000 stake, several players now had $3,000 or
more.

I moved my minimum bet to Player. Bank won.

Same story for the fourth and fifth hands.

Worse, I lost track of my resolve. I decided I had to
bet more than the $100 minimum just to catch up and
get into a competing position.

I lost hand after hand. By the eleventh hand, when
ordinarily I would have begun my real play, all I had in
front of me was $600. I bet it all on Player. I was dealt
a natural 8.

The bank turned over 9.

I was the second player to be knocked out of the
game.

They had to chase me to give me my $1,000 prize
check.

Carole joined me in the pit after I left the table. She
insisted I watch the rest of the game.

In the next eighteen hands, *there were five more Ties!*
And there were several players who bet $200 on Tie
each time! This gave them $8,000 in additional win-
nings and $2,600 in losses for a balance of $5,400.

It was also a very lopsided Bank shoe. Bank won fifteen hands while Player only won eight.

I've remarked earlier that to double your money gives
you a fighting chance for the big prize. To triple it is

ordinarily a sure thing.

Not today, Josephine.

By the last few hands, there were players sitting with $16,000, $22,000, and $24,000.

Instead of resorting to a holding position, they were betting the maximum $2,000 on each hand. The person who was so far ahead that he couldn't be beaten if he now played minimums continued to bet $2,000 a hand. He finished second. Second prize was $20,000.

Thoughtful playing would have given him another $80,000.

I realized that I wouldn't have been in the final race because that isn't the way I play. Can you imagine sitting down at an ordinary baccarat table with $2,000 and having $24,000 after two dozen hands? Ah, if life were only like that!

So the challenge is there.

I'm still determined to win my third tournament.

Winning A Million Dollars!

Of all the baccarat tournaments I've played in or observed, there were two that offered a top prize of $1 million. Second prize was $150,000.

Here, a $10,000 entry fee was required, and this one wasn't waived for anyone.

The mathematics was interesting. Entry fees alone gave the casino $1,560,000. This covered the casino cost of prizes and rather nice gifts for each entrant.

I was knocked out in the second round of the one in which I played. In retrospect, I didn't play well.

It was fascinating to watch the action in the final round.

A heavily bearded gentleman from another country who apparently spoke no English became a steady winner and soon was so far ahead of everyone else at the table that he seemed to have the million-dollar first prize locked up.

Then an insane scenario began. At the opposite side of the table, an attractive woman in her twenties began to make sizable wagers.

All the bearded gentleman had to do was either place minimum bets or shadow the woman.

Instead, he seemed to have a compulsion to bet against her.

If she bet Bank, he bet Player. Both were betting maximum $2,000 bets. If she bet Player, he bet Bank.

Again and again, she won and he lost.

When it was over, she called to her father who was a spectator, "Daddy, get mother over here *now!* I've just won a million dollars!"

And indeed she had.

YOUR BEST
SHOT

Minimums and maximums change constantly.

I report some specifics in this book. Since the gaming scene changes daily, you must check on the current situation. Casinos are bought by new owners. People change. Rules change. Regulations change.

Few things last. Only one thing remains constant: *the per*. That's there to chop you down every time you give it enough opportunity.

In the beginning, Atlantic City casinos set out to become grind joints. They were content to take a little money from a lot of people. Bus 'em in, make 'em happy, separate 'em from their savings or pension checks or welfare checks.

Competition and the high cost of attracting hordes of people convinced owners that they had to also seek the high roller. As a general rule, big players equal big losers.

For a long time, the only big-money baccarat games were on the Las Vegas Strip. That's changed. Now you can find major action in downtown Las Vegas as well as the posh Strip hotels that offer you a chance to bet $100,000 a hand.

Benny "Doc" Binion, father of the clan, often boasted that he strove to "give a gambler a good shot." And, indeed, he did, a tradition that his family carries on.

The Horseshoe has a $50,000-per-hand limit at baccarat.

Downtown Vegas is also the place where you can practice the game for small change. At the El Cortez, the minimum bet is $5, as it is in most other downtown sawdust joints. But at the California Club, you can play for as little as $2 a hand.

Slogans like "Play With Your Head, Not Over It" have never stopped anyone from being hurt because they wagered and lost too much at the tables or at the slots. That's why my most valuable gambling advice is *Don't.*

However if you're going to ignore my advice, then select your opponent, be it the slot machine or the blackjack table or the craps table or the baccarat pit.

Never carry more cash in your pockets than you're prepared to lose.

Never play a game (or a machine) that you don't thoroughly understand.

If you win money and are smart enough to depart gambling town, never return with more than half of what you won.

Better advice I couldn't give my wife or children.

A Different Perspective on Winners

A casino owner I know likens his casino to a store that "sells" bets. And like the shop that markets shoes or shirts at a profit, the casino, to survive, must "sell" its bets at a profit.

In other words, this man insists that casinos don't win their money. They earn it.

Okay. That's not revolutionary thinking, is it?

Now comes the good part. This fellow also says that casinos *do not* earn their money from losers, but rather from *winners*!

He explains it this way: a player makes a $1,000 bet at craps. He loses. The customer didn't pay anything for the bet.

The casino, says the casino owner, should consider the $1,000 it collected merely as money to be held in escrow. Another player will come along and bet $1,000 on the craps table and win.

Ah, but when he wins, the casino gives him only $1,000.

"What's wrong with that?" you may ask.

What's wrong is that if he were paid the true odds, he would be given approximately $1,028. This customer "paid" $28 for his bet.

Let me quote further from this unusual casino owner philosophy:

"Simply winning a guy's money in the casino doesn't give me any real satisfaction because that's just luck. I'm gambling, and I can't rely on it. The only thing I can rely on is what I earn, not what I win. What I happen to win on any given day is only in escrow, and every casino's the same way. They only rely on what they earn from the house edge—that tiny .414 percent or .846 percent on the craps table; that 5.26 percent on the roulette table; and so forth. [The European version with its single "0" cuts the percentage against you to 2.7 percent.]

"Here's another way of thinking about the house edge. When a guy makes a flat bet of $1,000 on the craps table, I make $14 on that bet, whether he wins or loses. I've got $14 in an imaginary escrow account. It's going to stay there, and I'm going to be able to bank that money someday as sure as the sun is going to come up tomorrow.

"If he makes ten bets at $1,000 a bet, that's $140 I earn. If he *wins* all ten bets, I will earn $140. He's ahead $10,000, but in actuality, he's stuck 140 bucks, because that's what those bets really cost him."

When you win money in a casino, you've earned it. It's time to stop thinking about it as "their money," and as I've told you many times in these pages, it's time to run, not walk, to the nearest transportation home.

Stuart's Seven Rules For Beating Baccarat

1. Never gamble when you're tired.
2. Never gamble when you're unhappy.
3. Never forget that the only way you will walk away with winnings is if you walk away. Leave while you're ahead. Don't challenge Lady Luck by sitting too long.
4. Never buck bad luck. If things aren't going well with you, stand up and wander away. You can always return. The game goes on. They will still be playing it years after you and I are dead.
5. Never buck a trend. If Player or Bank side wins three consecutive times, remember my Rule of Three. Bet on the winning side, or don't bet.

6. Always remember that baccarat is a "heads or tails" game. Don't lose your head. Else you'll have a tale that shouldn't be told!
7. Never forget that the casino depends on you to lose the struggle to control yourself. Fool them! Hit and run!

And may Dame Luck smile on you all the days of your life!

Remembrance of Shoes Past

A collection of scorecards from some of the more memorable shoes I have played at various casinos—with appropriate comments.

I had a "belly hunch" here and bet tie on the first hand
and won! This shoe turned out to be a winner for me
because Bank and Player wins seemed to even out. Then
Bank moved a little ahead, so I switched to Player and
won six out of a seven-hand run.

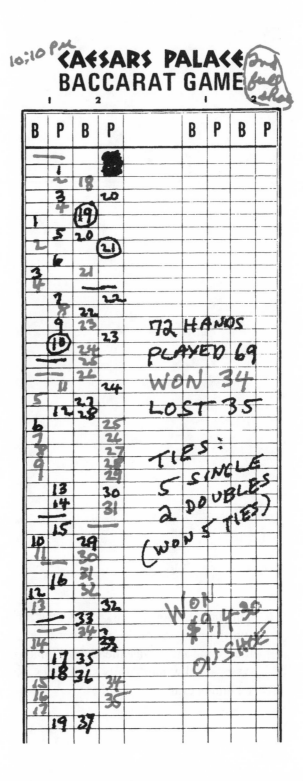

10:10 PM

CAESARS PALACE
BACCARAT GAME

72 HANDS
PLAYED 69
WON 34
LOST 35

TIES:
5 SINGLE
2 DOUBLES
(WON 5 TIES)

WON
$9,430
ON SHOE

This partial shoe is marked five, but it actually was the
fourth of the series. In other words, I had been sitting
there too long. I was ahead, but found that I was losing
wagers and winning only small ones. Rather than see the
winnings evaporate, I quit.

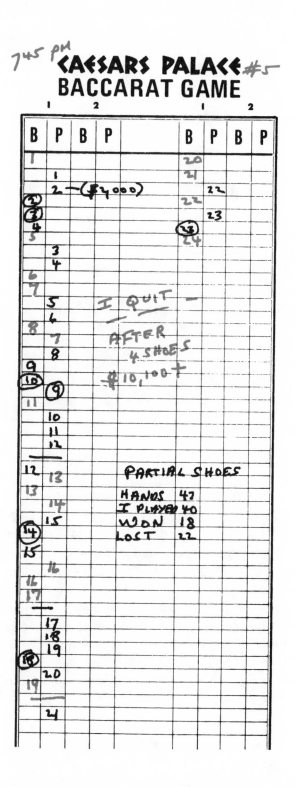

745 pm

CAESARS PALACE #5
BACCARAT GAME

	1		2			1		2	
B	P	B	P		B	P	B	P	
1					20				
	1				21				
	2	— ($4,000)				22			
②					22				
③						23			
4					㉓				
5					24				
	3								
	4								
6									
7									
	5		I QUIT —						
	6								
8			—						
	7		AFTER						
	8		4 SHOES						
9									
⑩	⑨		$10,100+						
11									
	10								
	11								
	12								
12	13		PARTIAL SHOES						
13			HANDS 47						
	14		I PLAYED 40						
	15		WON 18						
⑭			LOST 22						
15									
	16								
16									
17									
	17								
	18								
	19								
⑱									
	20								
19									
	21								

I was a $10,000 loser when I sat down at this shoe. The ninth Bank win gave me $4,000, and I reduced the next bet to $3,000 and jumped up again to $4,000 with the eleventh Bank win and stayed at that level until the fifth Player had killed the streak. At 95 cents to my dollar, I won $18,050 even though I lost $4,000 when the fifth Player came along. Suddenly I felt unsure, so I sat out several hands. I began to realize how lucky I had been. But I lost five out of the next six hands that I bet on. I was delighted with my $25,000 turnaround, and I had a strong impulse to run. I wanted to stand up, leave the baccarat pit, and hurry back to my room. I did.

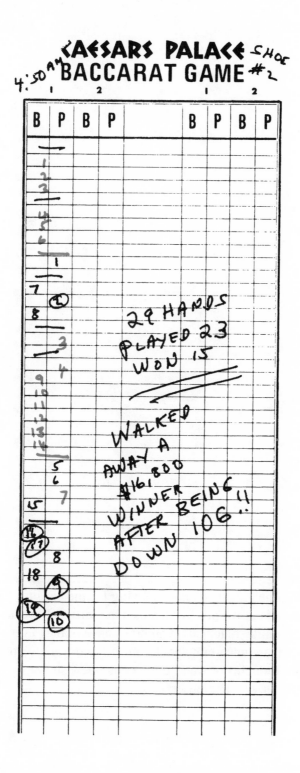

CAESARS PALACE
BACCARAT GAME

4:50 AM   SHOE #2

29 HANDS
PLAYED 23
WON 15

WALKED
AWAY A
$161,800
WINNER
AFTER BEING
DOWN 106!!

This one reflects unusual playing for me because I actually sat out twenty-five hands. One virtue of baccarat is that, unlike blackjack, you don't have to play every hand. If you are uncertain about yourself and want to collect your thoughts or want to map out a new strategy, you need only sit and observe.

3 PM

Tropicana
HOTEL AND COUNTRY CLUB
Baccarat score card

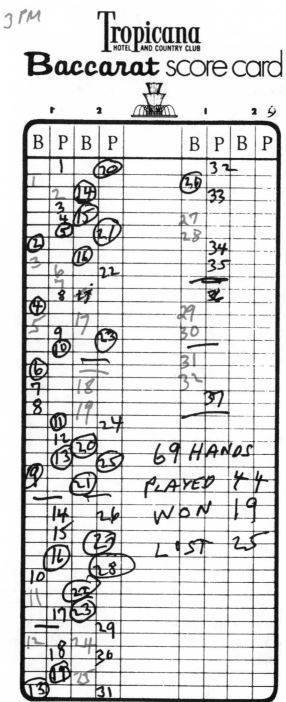

B	P	B	P		B	P	B	P
		1	20			32		
1		2	14		26			
		3	15			33		
		4			27			
2		5	21		28			
3			16			34		
		6	22			35		
		7				36		
		8	23					
4			17		29			
5		9			30			
		10	13					
6					31			
7			18		32			
8			19			37		
11			24					
		12						
		13	20					
			25					
9			21					
		14	26					
		15						
		16	27					
			28					
10			22					
11			23					
		17						
			29					
12		18	24					
			30					
		19	25					
13			31					

69 HANDS
PLAYED 44
WON 19
LOST 25

This is another example of having been lucky. When the shoe came to me, I made seven passes. After that, as I lost more wagers than I won, I decided to follow my own philosophy. I had hit, and now I ran.

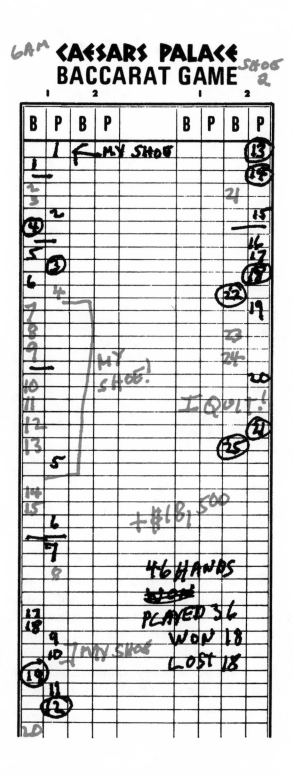

This shoe started out like gangbusters when I won six out
of the first seven hands I played. It seemed so strongly a
Bank shoe that I stubbornly stuck to Bank for the next
six hands, but only won two of them. Despite this, I did
win a disproportionate thirty-eight hands to the thirty-
three I lost, so I was a money winner, thanks exclusively
to the fact that I won six of the last eight hands.

7:50 AM CAESARS PALACE
BACCARAT GAME

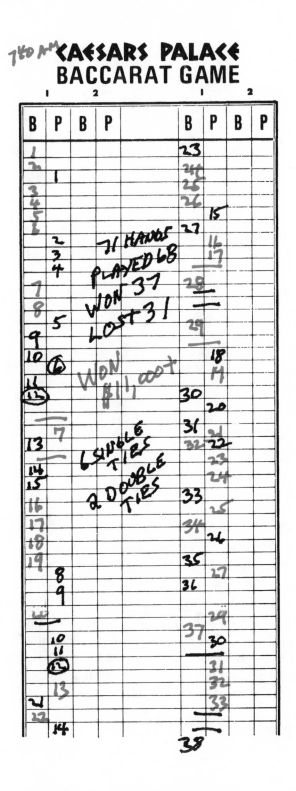

This is one case where I should have stayed in bed.
When Bank hit eighteen to Player's twelve, I assumed
that things would even out. In gaming, as in life, take
nothing for granted. The shoe ended up forty-four to
twenty-nine. I was stubborn, tired, and dumb. For example, after the Bank won its thirty-ninth hand, I failed to
follow my own Rule of Three. I should have bet Bank or
not bet at all. Instead, I stubbornly made three more
Player bets, and they cost me a bundle. I see that I have
written on top of this one "Disaster Card!"

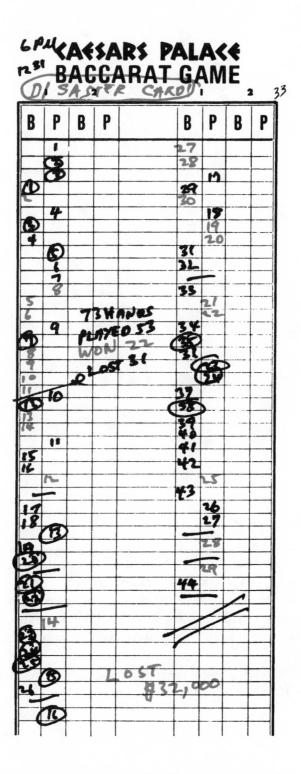

Of the seventy-nine hands that had decisions, I played
sixty-seven. I won thirty-six and lost thirty-one.
This was a lovely shoe because it was spiced with
streaks. I made a killing when the Bank side won six
consecutive hands. There were also three sequences of
five.
Winning five more hands that I lost gave me a "go home
now" gift of $23,000.

P	B	P	B	P	B	P	B
⌇			⑫		25		35
	①		⑬	16		26	
1			⑭	17		—	
	2	10		18			36
2			15	19			37
3			16	20			38
4			17			27	
	3		18		26	28	
	4		19		㉗		39
5		11			28	29	
	5			21			40
	6		⑳		29		41
	7	12			30		42
	8	—		22			㊸
	9	13			31		㊹
	10		21		32	30	
6			22		33	31	
7		14			㉞		45
8		15		㉓		32	
⑨			23	24			46 47
	⑪		24	25			-1

"BET WITH YOUR HEAD, NOT OVER IT"

TC/Pit 021 Rev. 2/88

There was nothing very unusual or very bad about this shoe except the way I played it. Although the longest streaks were four for the Bank and four for Player, there were plenty of threes and twos. When it was all over, I had just been unlucky.

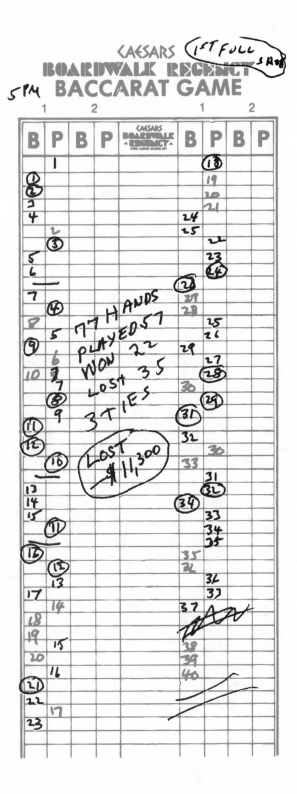

CAESARS (1ST FULL SR8)

BOARDWALK REGENCY
5PM BACCARAT GAME

77 HANDS
PLAYED 57
WON 22
LOST 35
3 TIES

LOST $11,300

I lost two hands more than I won on this shoe.
Fortunately, my loss was only $2,200. That was largely
due to the fact that I won my last three bets. (At that
point, I was betting big to recover.) I made seven passes
when I got the shoe, and someone else had made eight
passes earlier. Nevertheless, I wasn't betting enough on
the hands I won, and I was losing too many of the spo-
radic large bets. Note that here I was true to my preach-
ing. The eleventh and twelfth Bank wins were hands I
didn't play. I figured this was going to be 2-2, 2-2 switch
shoe since there had been so many twos up above, so on
the thirteenth Bank win, I was on Player. But that had
been three times for the Bank, so my choice was either to
bet Bank or not to bet at all. I bet Bank and won five of
the next six hands.

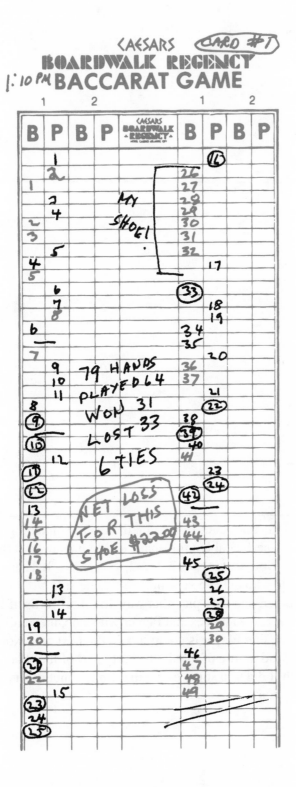

Uutil the thirteenth Bank win, there was something so design-perfect about this that I had to include it in this book. Note that it runs 2-2, 2-2, 1-1, 3-3, 1-1. There are people who believe very much that one side will imitate the other, and they play that way. In other words, if Bank has made two passes and Player wins one, they will assume that Player is going to win the next one. Note that I did a little of that in the early part of the shoe. As a result, I did win some hands that I might not otherwise have won.

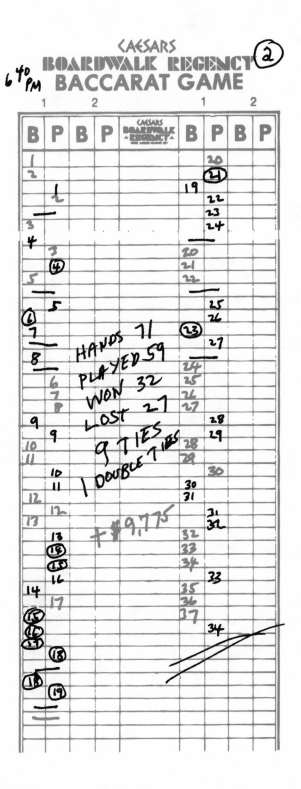

CAESARS
BOARDWALK REGENCY ②
BACCARAT GAME

6⁴⁰ PM

	1		2			1		2	
B	**P**	**B**	**P**	CAESARS BOARDWALK REGENCY	**B**	**P**	**B**	**P**
1						20			
2					19	㉑			
	1					22			
	2					23			
3						24			
4									
	3				20				
	④				21				
5					22				
	5					25			
⑥						26			
7				㉓		27			
8		HANDS 71			24				
		PLAYED 59			25				
	6	WON 32			26				
	7				27				
	8	LOST 27				28			
9						29			
	9	9 TIES			28				
10		1 DOUBLE TIES			28				
11						30			
	10				30				
	11				31				
12						31			
13	12	+ $9,775				32			
	13				32				
	⑭				33				
	⑮				34				
	16					33			
14					35				
	17				36				
⑮					37				
⑯						34			
	⑱								
⑱	⑲								

I was certainly out of sync with this shoe. By the time the fifty-third hand had been played, I was out $18,000. At least I had the good sense to get up and move. Note that of the last fourteen hands that were played while I sat at the table, I was able to win only three while losing eight.

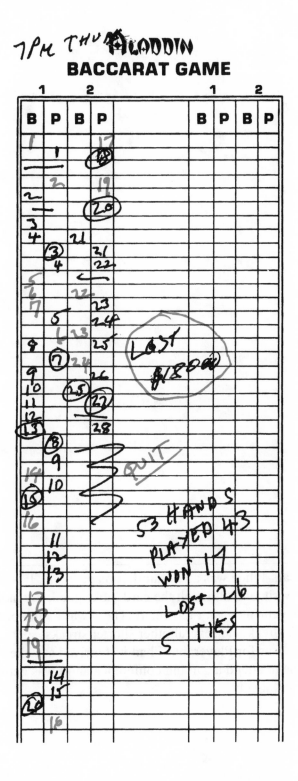

7PM THU ALADDIN
BACCARAT GAME

LOST
W/80@

QUIT

53 HANDS
PLAYED 43
WON 17
LOST 26
5 TIES

Caesars Tahoe was an unfamilier place to me. It was my
first visit, and although the card looks good, my money
management wasn't too smart. There was a nine-pass
Bank streak and several other shorter streaks, such as
six passes for Player, but I had just arrived at Lake
Tahoe to attend a gaming conference and I was betting
conservatively.

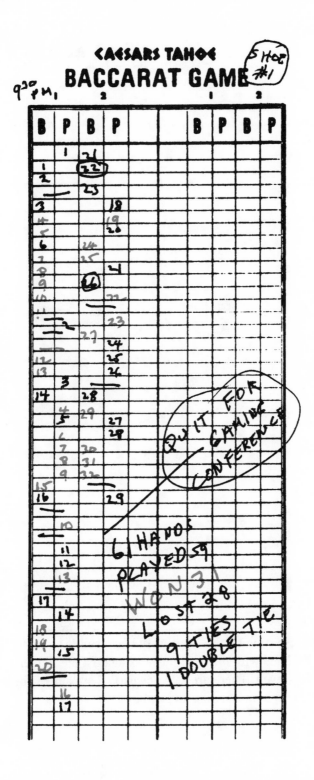

I'm reporting on this shoe only because it's so typical.
Bank ends with thirty-eight wins against the Player's
thirty-seven. There are two occasional streaks of four, but
mostly it's ones, twos, and threes.

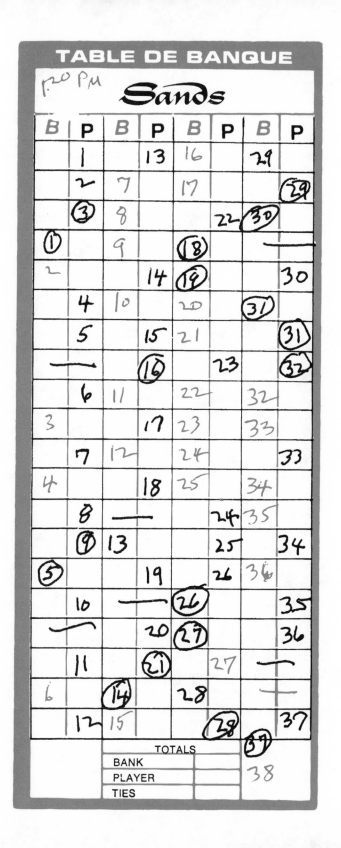

This shoe was every player's dream. The scorecard
reflects the fact that I lost seven hands and won only
three of the first ten on which I gambled. It didn't look
promising.

Then Dame Fortune stroked me. Starting with Bank hand
twenty-one, I won seven in a row. Bank hand # thirty-
seven gave me the beginning of another winning six. The
last three of these were at $8,000 each.

This was a highly profitable shoe for me even though I
won only two more hands than I lost. I played sixty-four,
won thirty-three, and lost thirty-one.

If only they all ended like this one!

TRUMP'S CASTLE

P	B	P	B	P	B	P	B
—		8		(20)		25	
	1		13	21			34
	2	9		22			35
1			14	23		(26)	
	3	10		24		—	
2			15	25			36
3		11		26		—	
	(4)			27		27	
	5	12		21			37
	6	13		22			38
4			16	—		—	
	(7)	14			28		39
	8		17		29		40
	(9)	15			30		41
—		16		23		—	
	10	17			31		42
	11	18		—		—	
5			18	24			
6			19		32		
	12		20		33	(18)	
7		19		—			𝒥

"BET WITH YOUR HEAD, NOT OVER IT"

TC/Pit 021 Rev. 2/88

Another of those hands I label "freekoes." Bank won
forty-three to Player's thirty-two. I didn't lose a lot of
money with this one because there were a few streaks
that I caught, but I wasn't happy with the shoe. It can be
dangerous when the cards swing too heavily in either
direction.

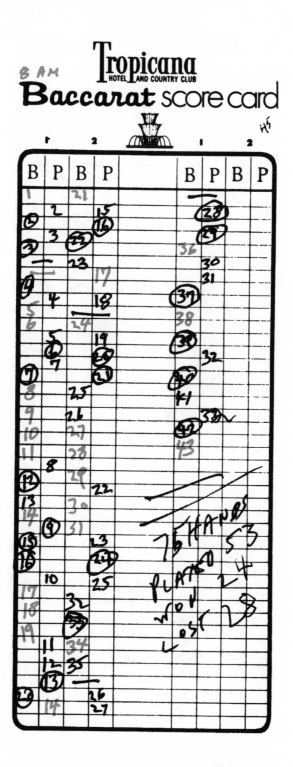

Another "disaster" hand. I won twenty hands while losing thirty-two and I was betting for pretty high stakes.
One of the things that saved me was that after Player had
won three bets, I knew I had to bet with Player or not bet
at all. The three Player bets that I won were for substantial money and reduced an even larger loss, although losing $18,200 in a half hour is not nearly as much fun as
winning that much!

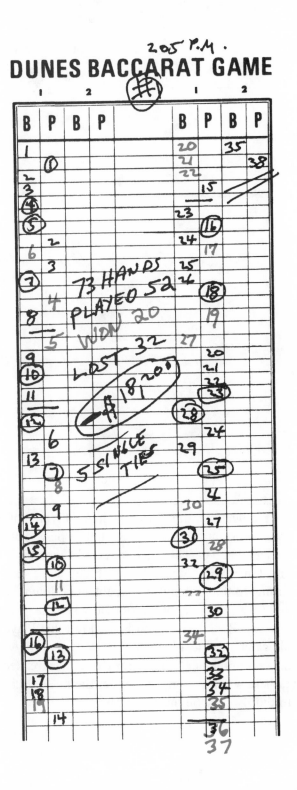

DUNES BACCARAT GAME

2:05 P.M.

I didn't indicate on this card how much I won, but my win was substantial for the three shoes I played at Tropicana that day. This shoe reflected "unnatural" results. Forty Bank wins to thirty-three Player's is not according to the probability percentages. Note that I caught several streaks of threes, and when the score was twenty-two Bank to sixteen Player, I felt that Player would catch up. I lost the next bet, betting on Player, and then I sat out the next one. After Bank had streaked with four, there was no choice but to bet Bank. Good thing that I did! Bank won the next three.

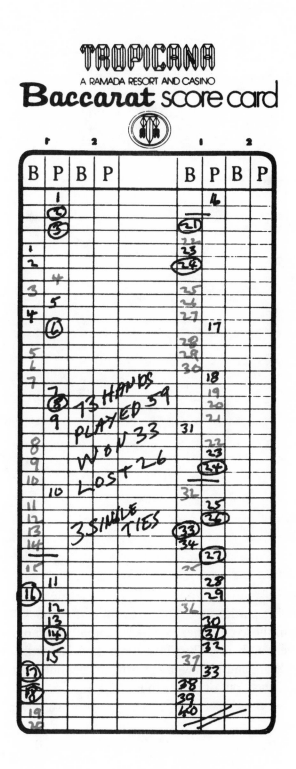

TROPICANA
A RAMADA RESORT AND CASINO
Baccarat score card

B	P	B	P		B	P	B	P
	1					4		
	⊘				21			
	⑤							
1					22			
2					23			
					24			
3	4				25			
	5				26			
4					27			
	⑥					17		
					28			
5					29			
6					30			
7						18		
	7	13 HANDS				19		
	⑧	PLAYED 59				20		
	9	WON 33			31	21		
8					22			
9		LOST 26			23			
10					34			
	10				32			
11					35			
12	3 SINGLE TIES				36			
13					33			
14					34			
15					27			
					36			
⑪	11				28			
	12				29			
	13				36			
	⑭				30			
	15				31			
					32			
⑰					37			
⑱					33			
					38			
19					39			
20					40			

This is a partial shoe. I try to avoid partial shoes. This is
one of those rare ones in which I actually won money! I
started out badly. Then I was on a Bank streak that put
me ahead, and I knew it was time to "get out of town."
Or, at least, out of the casino.

MGM GRAND HOTEL BACCARAT GAME

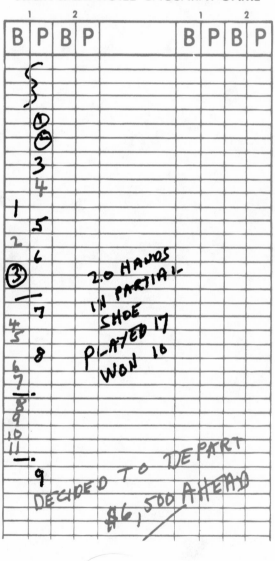

	1		2				1		2	
B	P	B	P			B	P	B	P	

2.0 HANDS
IN PARTIAL
SHOE
PLAYED 17
WON 16

DECIDED TO DEPART
$6,500 AHEAD